Advance Praise for
Millennials' Guide to Getting Your S#!t Together

"As a Millennial, I know our generation is seeking to understand ourselves and grow toward healthy and fulfilling lives. *Millennials' Guide to Getting Your S#!t Together* is an excellent handbook in doing just that. It includes practical advice on figuring out who you are, dealing with your childhood, how to make sense of friendships and work, and how to face the future. Authors Sphoorti and Jennifer give non-judgmental, grounded guidance, which helps readers think more deeply about their purpose and personal goals."

-Valerie Weaver, LCSW-NY, RSW-MB, Licensed Clinical Social Worker

"I had no problem diving into *Millennials' Guide to Getting Your S#!t Together* I simply eyed the chapters that appeal to me at this point in my life (something like 20 chapters), and gave myself time and space to take notes. I found the advice given was easy to follow and that I certainly have areas where, as the title suggests, I can get my s#!t together."

-Daniel Cruz Lattimore, PhD, NCC, Millennial

"*Millennials' Guide to Getting Your S#!t Together* is an easy guide to life as an adult! This book covers a wide range of topics that can be hard to figure out as an adult in today's world, especially when we lack mentorship. This book is a self-guided journey to better your life and get you thinking!"

-Dawn Taylor, Trauma Specialist, The Taylor Way

MILLENNIALS' GUIDE TO

GETTING YOUR S#!T TOGETHER

What No One Ever Told You About Adulting

WINDING PATHWAY BOOKS

Sphoorti Pandit-Kerr

Jennifer P. Wisdom

Published by Winding Pathway Books

WINDING PATHWAY BOOKS

ISBN (print): 978-1-954374-13-3
ISBN (e-book): 978-1-954374-14-0

Book design by Wendy C Garfinkle
Cover design by Brian Sisco, 115 studios llc, and Wendy C Garfinkle
Sphoorti's Photo Credit: Forrest Pandit-Kerr
Jennifer's Photo Credit: Diego G. Diaz

For more information or bulk orders, visit www.millennialsguides.com

Printed in the United States of America

Contents

HOW TO USE THIS BOOK

If you've read other books in the *Millennials' Guides* series (*Millennials' Guide to Work, Millennials' Guide to Management and Leadership, Millennials' Guide to Relationships,* or *Millennials' Guide to Workplace Politics)*, you know how this works. *Millennials' Guides* are not books necessarily best read cover to cover. We encourage you to review the table of contents and identify a challenge you are currently having or recently experienced. Turn to those pages to start finding a solution!

Each chapter includes a brief description, several things to think about, and activities that you may want to try. Many times, you can feel improvement after trying one option. You'll see some information repeated across different chapters because they're likely to be helpful for many problems. For complex challenges, you may want to attempt several interventions at the same time.

It's important to have patience and give the solutions and considerations a little bit of time to work. Some ideas that you try won't solve the problem but will make it a little better or make you think differently about the issue -- that's still success! If you don't feel comfortable trying an activity, try something else. Some of the activities are very low risk, such as changing your expectations of other people. Others can appear more challenging, such as directly discussing a concern with a family member, friend, or colleague. Start with actions that feel like lower risk to you and work your way up to more challenging actions.

As you work through the book, you'll get better at understanding yourself, reading situations, responding respectfully to people in your life, building a positive and diverse support network, and applying solutions effectively. Observe, be patient, clarify your own boundaries, and learn. The more you know what you want, the more you'll be able to achieve your goals. If you're not sure what you want, that's okay too--that's a perfect place to be while you're in your 20s and 30s (and even your 40s!). The goal of the strategies in this book is to help you develop skills that will serve you well as you continue to move forward in your lifelong exploration of the life you want to live.

Each of you reading this book is a unique person with talents to share with the world. Our hope is that this book can make it easier for you to do so. Good luck improving the world!

Part I. How Do I Start Getting My S#!t Together?

Chapter 1: Who Am I?

You may think that you have no control over your world or at the organization where you work. Not so! Not only do you impact your culture, but it is important to remember that you are a *part* of the culture in your world -- a very important part! *Who you are* shapes the culture around you. But first things first: do you know who you are?

1. **Often individuals, especially young people, feel that they have little to no say in the structure, environment and overall character of their world** or the organization for which they work. Know that your voice is important, and you *can* impact the culture of your organization. Knowing who you are, and how you show up in multiple roles in different groups, can increase your impact in the world.

2. **Everyone has multiple aspects of their identity.** Identities may include ethnic, racial, national, gender, regional, sexual, personal, and organizational identities. These identities interact with each other, making you unique. Some parts of your identity you were born with (nationality, ethnicity). Others may change over time (group membership, religion, political affiliation). Who you are today is a result of countless interactions over time in which you discover who you are and how you fit into the world. What are some of your identities? These may be as a son or daughter, Puerto Rican, lesbian, child of immigrants, Muslim, New Yorker, or many more. Write down your current identities.

3. **Within the world, you are part of a larger group.** In fact, you're part of several larger groups. You are a part of your family, your community, social organizations, political clubs, professional organizations, religious groups, a generation, and more. Even sports teams and social media groups count. And of course, your workplace. Write down a list of the various

groups or organizations to which you belong, starting with your family.

4. **For the identities that you weren't born into, you have various ways of identifying how you fit into other groups.** These can include considering how you became a part of the groups you now affiliate with, increasing our awareness about the nature and history of those affiliations and identities, understanding rituals or rites of passage associated with these groups, attending events with others in this identity to build affiliation, and more. How you become affiliated with these groups can vary widely, from completing a membership form to apply to an organization, attending a ceremony or ritual and sticking with it, or a more formal initiation ceremony.

5. **Because society changes, along with the groups which make up our society, identities change as well.** Thinking back to when you were a child, how has your identity changed over the years? Have various parts of your identity become more important or less important over time? Are there parts of your identity that you would like to be more prominent or less prominent?

6. **Each of the groups you listed has its own values, norms, and expectations,** which can be written, but more often, are unwritten. They're simply "known" – or in many cases, they are assumed to be known by all. Pick one of the groups that you belong to, and identify any values, norms, and expectations that may be written down. Then consider what values, norms, and expectations you believe the group shares that are not written down. Note these may be different from the written ones. These can include how the group determines its membership, how people treat outsiders, how members treat each other, how decisions are made, and more. Once you have a good list, share the list with a trusted other member of the group and see if you are in agreement.

7. **Once you have a sense of the values, norms, and expectations of a group,** identify whether you agree with them. Are they applied consistently and fairly to all members? What happens when members have different behavior or attitudes that conflict with the values, norms, and expectations in place? Do you think that the members of these groups are open to new ideas? Why or why not?

8. **How a group treats outsiders is an often-overlooked indicator of the group's values.** Often members within a group feel comfortable with one another so they feel that they can make remarks about outsiders that may seem harmless. Ethnic jokes, jokes about women or jokes about LGBTQ individuals might not seem like a big deal, but they are really the first level of prejudice. Have you ever heard others in any of your groups make such remarks? If so, how might that change the values, norms, and expectations you wrote down above? If you've heard such comments before, how did others respond? How would you handle the situation if you heard someone in one or more of your groups using disparaging remarks or jokes about outsiders?

9. **Once you've written down this information,** hold on to it. We'll return to it later in the book. Feel free to update it as you need to, and to discuss it with others. And congratulations -- you've made a huge step forward in understanding who you are and how you fit in the world!

See Also:
Chapter 6: Thinking Long Term
Chapter 10: Understanding Your Own Thoughts
Chapter 19: Goal Setting

Chapter 2: What Are You Struggling With: Is It You, Or Is It Them?

Sometimes we're in a great place in our lives and it seems like everything is working well. For all those other times, well, you have this book. It's important to understand what things are working and what things are not working well for us.

1. **Take an inventory: what's working and what's not working?** Even just five minutes can be helpful. Consider major life areas such as your career, finances, education, relationships, physical health, emotional and mental health, your attitude/perspective, and anything else you can consider. Even if you feel like a mess, that's okay. Write down what's working and what's not working.

2. **What does it mean to have your shit together?** If you did have your shit together, what would be different about your life? If you know people with their shit together, what is it about them that lets you know they've got it together?

3. **What do you want to be different?** Try the magic wand test: If you had a magic wand that would make you instantly have your shit together, how would your life be different than it is right now? Pay attention to those changes. We can't change our height, or our age, but there's a whole lot else we can change.

4. **Maybe it's them?** "Before you diagnose yourself with depression or low self-esteem, first make sure you are not, in fact, surrounded by assholes." Sometimes we're surrounded by assholes, and we don't even realize it. The term "asshole" refers to stupid, irritating, or mean people

who do not bring value to our lives. This includes constant complainers, whiners, blamers, gaslighters, and narcissists. If you realize you're surrounded by assholes, start working on an escape plan immediately!

See also:
Chapter 4: Building a Support Team
Chapter 6: Thinking Long-Term
Chapter 19: Goal Setting

Chapter 3: Assessing Your Strengths

We all have strengths; and everyone's strengths are different. It takes all kinds to make this world. Some strengths are more useful that others in getting your shit together in the society we live in. Knowing your strengths can help you best identify which ones will help you work towards your goals. Here are some ways to get better acquainted with your strongest qualities.

1. **Work on knowing yourself.** Self-awareness is one of the most useful qualities we can develop. A thorough and honest assessment of yourself will help identify what skills serve you best in any situation

2. **Think about tasks you've done well at in the past.** Which parts of the task went swimmingly? Which parts felt harder than others? Thinking through these will help specifics of your strengths, not just general skills.

3. **Reflect on situations you felt you handled well.** Was it the way you communicated with the people involved? Was it the environment you worked in? Was it the people with you worked with? Identifying what factors made something work well is helpful in knowing your strengths and knowing when to use them.

4. **Situational awareness.** Read the room. Knowing what is needed in any given scenario helps hone your strengths and awareness of what will serve you well to navigate it. Different qualities can be a strength depending on the situation.

5. **Ask for feedback.** It can be hard for us to objectively view ourselves. Getting feedback from people who are vested in our progress can provide a unique perspective on our strengths.

Qualities we might not even be aware of might be our greatest assets. When I (SPK) first started intentionally asking for feedback from coworkers and supervisors in professional settings, it was difficult to accept it. It is human nature to be defensive of our actions and beliefs, and receiving critical feedback from people who I knew cared about me and my progress allowed me to really work through the negative feelings and focus on the useful advice I was given.

6. **Learn from your mistakes.** It is human to make mistakes. Learning from errors we make helps us work on ourselves in areas that could use some support or development.

7. **Knowing your limitations.** Knowing your limitations is a strength! This goes hand in hand with self-awareness.

8. **Getting support with weaknesses.** Just like it is human to make mistakes, it is human to ask for support. We often have people with complementary strengths that help us identify and work on aspects of ourselves that could benefit with some support.

9. **Recognize that knowing and assessing your strengths in a continuous process.** We are ever changing as humans, and it is important to touch base with yourself and know that strengths and values can change as we grow and learn.

See also:
Chapter 1: Who Am I?
Chapter 17: Taking Stock of Your Influences
Chapter 43: Coming to Terms With Your History

Chapter 4: Building a Support Team

Today we all need support to get by in this crazy mixed-up world. Success is often a group effort – it really does take a village! Support can come in all forms – it could be a friend, parent, sibling, teacher, coach, and yes, even your beloved pets. A good support system is the key to success in any situation that you might face, but just how well do you know how to build that type of support system? Your team? Support that will be there regardless? It can be helpful to know your allies and build a support group of people who care about you and your progress.

1. **Know what you want and need from a support system.** Is it validation? A safe space to vent? Constructive feedback? Figuring out the purpose of your support system will help guide you in developing it.

2. **Identify people who share your value system.** People who value the same things that you do may have similar thought processes and can offer a validating and supportive space.

3. **Embrace your hobbies.** Connect with others who enjoy similar activities as you to build up your social network. This can be through volunteering, social clubs, Meetup groups or events of your interest.

4. **Expand your professional network.** Build relationships with coworkers within your organization. Broadening your network with other professionals in your field of work can help provide both learning and advancement opportunities.

5. **Work on deepening relationships with friends and family who you trust.** People who have your best interests at heart,

who respect you, and who make you feel positive and optimistic are a great foundation for a strong support system.

6. **Develop your own personal support process.** This could include self-care, ways of winding down after a day, activities you do to recharge or relax.

7. **It's okay to ask for help.** While you don't want to overwhelm the people who are there for you, it is absolutely okay to clarify what kind of support you need.

8. **Recognize that you can have different supports for different reasons and situations.** Different people can be supportive in various contexts and having a diverse support group can help you feel less alone.

9. **Nurture your Support Team.** Support systems are like trees: They require nourishment and continued engagement. Having strong roots is helpful, but without ongoing nurturing they can wither and fade. Make sure to nurture those who support you when you can.

10. **Chances are, you might already have a support team in your life, and you just don't see it yet.** The next few steps are going to show you just how easy it is to build your support team or even build it up better than you currently have it.

11. **Create your own personal Support Team.**
    a. Write down the names of everyone positive in your social circle. These could be people you interact with on a daily basis, partners, friends, family, coaches, teammates, etc.
    b. Identify who has been a good support person for you. When you start facing a difficult decision in life, they are there to help dig you out and focus on the goal ahead.

c. Remember, the size of your support team does not matter. You could have 50 people or five. As long as you have someone in your corner, the number is not important.

d. By now you most likely have a list of at least 1-5 people that you can go to when you need help. Of course, it could be more than that. This is your Support Team. You can tell them they're part of your Support Team, but you don't have to! They are the ones that will be with you every inch of the way and won't turn back. Keep them close.

See also:
Chapter 6: Thinking Long-Term
Chapter 11: Online Support Groups
Chapter 38: Who To Surround Yourself With

Chapter 5: Emergencies

Emergencies will happen. It is just a part of life. Below are some strategies that might help reduce the distress and negative outcomes of those emergencies.

1. **Try to proactively plan for as much as you can.** Think about your routine. Identify places where emergencies can emerge and try to set up a process to deal with them before they come up. Doing trial runs can help with knowing what to anticipate.

2. **Have a plan B. And a plan C and D for good measure.** Knowing that you have a backup plan can help ease some of the anxiety that emergencies can induce.

3. **Be flexible.** Sometimes even the best laid plans can throw you a curveball. Be willing to change strategies if your solution doesn't seem to be helping.

4. **Stay in a mindset that helps you best problem solve.** For some, this might be staying as calm as much as possible in the moment. While this is easier said than done, panic and anxiety can be muddling and prevent us in identifying effective ways forward. Some others might thrive under pressure so help create an environment that is best supports your needs in the moment.

5. **Reach out to your support system.** Emergencies are great times to tap into your support network – a new perspective, a supportive hand on your shoulder, people to diffuse the burden, or even a hard to hear perspective can all be valuable in finding your bearings.

6.   **Remember that you are human!** Emergent situations come up. Things and plans go belly up. Even the best and most thorough planning may not be enough. Anxiety, tension, or panic are normal human responses to emergencies, and dealing with emergencies is stressful. Having compassion for yourself is important to keep moving forward.

7.   **Sometimes things will just not work out – and that is okay.** Use these situations as learning opportunities while processing any feelings that they might have risen from those situations.

See also:
Chapter 6: Thinking Long-Term
Chapter 19: Goal Setting
Chapter 25: Making Sense of the World Around You

Chapter 6: Thinking Long-Term

What does it mean to get your shit together over the course of your life? What do you hope your life will look like in the future? This section helps you consider what you're aiming for, which will lay the groundwork for how to get there.

1. **What do you want?** This one question is the key to just about everything. What you want your life to look like can include your career, finances, education, relationships, physical health, emotional and mental health, your attitude/perspective, and anything else you can consider. If you give yourself a chance to just brainstorm what you would like your life to look like in 10 or 20 years, what do you come up with?

2. **What does it mean to have your shit together?** I (JPW) somehow got the idea in my head as a kid that by the time people are, say, 30 years old, they have their shit together. I'm not sure where I got that idea, but it didn't take long after I turned 30 for that fantasy to fade away. If you did have your shit together, what would be different about your life? If you know people with their shit together, what is it about them that lets you know they've got it together? Think big – we're talking the rest of your life.

3. **Goals aligned with your core values are easier to stick with.** If you're not sure what you want out of life, consider your values. If you value "security," your goals might be associated with building a safe environment and home. If you value "adventure," your goals could be travel and fun oriented.

4. **It's also helpful to articulate the "why" behind your long-term goals so when it gets hard you can remind yourself.** What

makes this goal important to you? Why this goal and not another? Push yourself to be specific.

5. **Some people swear by vision boards.** This is a process of creating a poster or document that has images of what you are striving for, usually cut from magazines, or printed from online. You can display your dream house, a picture of a confident person, etc.

6. **What do you want to feel long term?** Sometimes people focus on specifics such as a three-bedroom house or a sporty red car; it's also helpful to consider how you'd like to feel. How do you want to feel about your job, about your social and romantic life, about your family, about the world? Keep writing…

7. **Try the "perfect day" exercise.** Give yourself 20 minutes and some quiet time to fantasize what a perfect day would look like for you. Start with when you open your eyes in the morning: what do you see? Where are you? Is anyone with you? What do you do when you get up? What kind of food, or exercise, or work or fun do you have? What kind of weather is it? Take 20 minutes and get as specific as possible. When you're finished, take some notes, and consider what you'd like to keep as part of your long-term vision.

8. **It's always a balance between generalities and specificities.** If you say you want two children, an older boy with brown hair and a younger girl with blonde hair … you're likely to be disappointed. But if you say you want children who are kind and funny, you're more likely to get what you're looking for. Paint your long-term vision with broad strokes instead of getting overly focused on superficial details.

9. **Not deciding is still making a decision.** You can decide you don't want to think through what you want long term or set goals; that choice a decision to float through life and see where takes you. That's a perfectly fine choice but be aware that it is still a choice.

10. **Write down your long-term goals and cherish them.** Think of them like mental seeds you've planted in how you'd like the future to unfold. Check in on your goals periodically. Make changes as you desire. The longer you live, the more exciting it is to look back and fondly remember your goals – as well as to see how many of them you've achieved!

See also:
Chapter 19: Goal Setting
Chapter 25: Making Sense of the World Around You
Chapter 33: When Situations Seem to Repeat Themselves

Part II. Self-Directed Methods/Self Help

Chapter 7: Journaling

Many people find it helpful to write down their thoughts or ideas or to draw about them. Journaling is an engaging way to document your thoughts and work through them.

1. **The first rule of journaling is there are no rules.** You can use any kind of book or online program. You can write daily or sporadically or anywhere in between. You can write in the first person ("Today I ...") or you can address them to someone real or imagined ("Dear Pookie, ..."). Journals are entirely for your benefit, entertainment, and growth.

2. **Journaling has numerous benefits,** including helping you manage anxiety, reduce stress, and cope with depression.

3. **Journaling helps you prioritize problems, fears, and concerns.** It helps you track how you feel on a regular basis so that you can recognize triggers and learn ways to better control them. Journaling also allows you to identify your negative thoughts toward yourself and an opportunity to create positive self-talk.

4. **Keep it private.** To feel comfortable sharing your thoughts and feelings, it's important you have a way to keep your journal private. There are locking journals, or locking drawers, or various other ways to ensure that you're the only one with eyes on your journal. If you want to share, that's fine, but it's totally up to you.

5. **Make it easy.** Keep a pen and paper handy all the time. When you want to write down your thoughts, you can. You could also tap your comments into your phone's memo app, or use a journaling app.

6. **Write or draw whatever you want.** Your journal doesn't need to follow any certain structure. It's your own private place to

discuss and create whatever you want to express your feelings. Let the words and ideas flow freely. Don't worry about spelling mistakes or what other people might think.

7. **To prompt or not to prompt?** Free writing can be fun, but it's also possible to respond to prompts, such as, "List three wishes you have for your future," or "What is something you regret and why?" You can find lists of writing prompts online.

8. **Try lists!** As lifelong list makers, our journals are also full of lists. "Things that are bugging me," or "What I'm looking forward to," or "Ten goals for the new year" are all winners.

9. **If you're just getting started, set a timer.** Take it slow and set a timer for 2 or 3 minutes to sit and write. Eventually you can set it for 10 or more minutes, or not even use a timer at all!

10. **Review periodically.** It's a good idea to occasionally go back and look at what you wrote. Even flipping through pages casually will give you a sense of what your recurring patterns are. A quick review might even inspire you to make some changes.

11. **Writing should be relaxing and cathartic.** Writing time as relaxation time. It's a time to de-stress and wind down. Write in a place that's relaxing and soothing, maybe with a cup of tea or coffee. Ideally, you happily anticipate the opportunity to journal. If writing isn't relaxing, try drawing or sketching or simply doodling.

See also:

Chapter 8: Therapy

Therapy is a collaborative process with talking and self-work with a trained professional that can help guide you through mental health concerns and emotional distress. It can be a useful tool to identify sources and patterns of behavior and trauma. Knowledge is power, and the therapeutic process is helpful in living a more fulfilled life with lower distress.

1. **Therapy is an additional support not a fix.** Therapy can be an incredibly helpful experience in working through trauma and other life experiences. That said, it is one of the steps in developing your toolkit. Coping skills learned during the therapeutic process need to be used outside of the hour-a-week therapy session in the rest of your life for them to be helpful in integrating them into your life in a meaningful way.

2. **Develop skills to help better process experiences.** Understanding your emotions, thoughts and feelings can be to increase your own self-awareness in how you experience events. Avoiding acknowledging feelings associated with any experience can lead them to fester. Sometimes negative feelings manifest in weird psychosomatic ways in your body if they are not processed. I (SPK) spent years having chronic migraines and insomnia because I did not take any time for self-reflection and taking the care I needed to work through traumatic experiences.

3. **Grow coping skills aligning with our values.** It is important to know your value system. Understanding what we place importance in and what are our driving motivations is important in identifying coping skills that align with those values. Coping skills are not necessarily useful if using them doesn't make you feel any better off than when you started.

4. **There are different types of therapy.** There are many different types of therapy available out there – Cognitive Behavioral Therapy (CBT), Psychotherapy, Dialectical Behavior Therapy (DBT), Acceptance and Commitment Therapy (ACT), etc. Each has its strengths and usefulness in different situations. Finding the type of therapy that is most useful in different situations can lead to a much better therapeutic experience.

5. **Go in with an open mind.** Therapy can be a challenging and potentially uncomfortable process. As humans, we tend to avoid negative emotions or experiences. While delving into processing any experience, it can be uncomfortable to acknowledge it and possibly re-live negative aspects of it. Therapy can take time to be effective so keeping moving forward and focused on your progress.

6. **Everyone has a different path with therapy.** There is not a single step-by-step guide for therapy that works with everyone. Everyone can have a different pace with their progress - their trauma, their history, their purpose for going to therapy, relationship with their therapist, coping skills that align with their values are all factors that can influence someone's therapeutic progress.

7. **Be patient with the process and with yourself.** Healing. Takes. Time. It is vital to be patient with the therapeutic process and with yourself while going through it. As people experience therapy in different ways, expecting therapy to help fix your problems quickly can lead to prematurely dismissing your positive progress.

8. **Pay attention to your instincts.** Therapy is not a one size fits all. Self-awareness during the process can help us identify how helpful therapy is being for you. Acknowledging the uncomfortable parts and questions why they make us the feel the way they do can help identify our own biases. For example

– does this feel uncomfortable because it is detrimental to my wellbeing, or is it because I don't like being challenged?

9. **Find the right fit.** It is important to trust your therapist. Just as there are different types of therapy, there are different types of therapists. Having an honest relationship with your therapist is incredibly important to having a safe and positive therapeutic experience.

10. **It is a continuous process.** For some people therapy can be lifelong. Our lives are not defined by singular experiences, rather is an ongoing collection of experiences. Therapy can be a continuous tool in how we process all experiences in life. However, that does not mean that you must be going to therapy all the time. While therapy sessions can be paused or started as needed, recognizing that the skills learnt can be used in any context they seem helpful can make therapy be integrated much more effectively into our lives.

11. **Being in therapy doesn't mean a lack of will power or indicate any weaknesses.** Therapy in no way indicates a weakness – just an additional support. Therapists are trained to help us develop our own skills – just as mechanics are trained to fix cars, IT technicians are trained to fix computers and doctors are trained to fix medical problems. Think of it as a cast helping your broken bone heal correctly – it is a support, provides guidance and can help hasten the healing process.

See also:
Chapter 2: What Are You Struggling With: Is It You Or Is It Them?
Chapter 4: Building a Support Team
Chapter 6: Thinking Long-Term

Chapter 9: Medication

People often have strong perspectives on medication as self-help. Some people swear by their anti-depressant or ADHD medication. Others medicate themselves with caffeine, nicotine, alcohol, cannabis, or other substances. And still others try to live a life free of all medications including caffeine, alcohol, and pain relievers. How you consider medication is up to you. Read on to see some considerations, and always check with your health care provider.

1. **Medication can be an additional form of support.** Just as taking a pain reliever for a headache or to reduce a fever can help the healing process move quicker or offer relief from symptoms, psychiatric medications (and over-the-counter self-medications like caffeine, alcohol, and nicotine) can work in a similar capacity with mental health symptoms.

2. **Medication is not a fix-it pill.** While medications have the potential to provide enormous relief, they do not always fix the root cause of the issue. They can provide relief from symptoms, help fortify your emotional and physical reserves, and provide time to figure out the actual issue.

3. **Taking medication does not indicate a lack of willpower.** While psychiatric medications may not be necessary in your healing process, taking medications does not indicate a weakness. Sometimes the purpose of medications is simply to provide relief from pain and allow you time to work through it and any associated negative experiences.

4. **Consider how you may self-medicate,** including caffeine, nicotine, alcohol, or other substances. Are you happy with how you are using these or other substances? Sometimes it's difficult to manage dosages or self-medicate; that might be a sign a consultation with a physician might be helpful.

5. **Medications can address chemical imbalances in the brain.** Sometimes medications can help address and correct main reason for any symptoms that you might be experiencing. In this case, these medications are acting to make up something that your body is unable to produce enough of on its own – much like an iron, or thyroid hormone supplement.

6. **Process of trial and error.** Finding the right prescription medication and dosage for you can take some time. It is important to be patient and understand that while medications can work quickly, some medications – particularly psychiatric medications -- have an adjustment period and can take up to 6 weeks or more to work their full effect.

7. **Listen to your body and advocate for yourself as needed.** Ultimately, you know your body best. If you feel that you have given a particular medication an adequate shot and it is still not working for you – speak up! Your healthcare providers are ultimately there to help you manage your care, and honest input from you about what is and isn't working will help them guide you through figuring out what is the best fit for you.

8. **Have a long-term plan with medications.** Identify what your goal is with respect to taking medications. Sometimes long-

term use of medications can have permanent effects on your body. Ensure you know all the aspects associated with a particular medication so you can make an effective long-term plan with them including how long you plan to take them, how your dose may be adjusted and if any, steps to be taken before potentially stopping a medication.

See also:
Chapter 4: Building a Support Team
Chapter 10: Understanding Your Own Thoughts, Feelings, and
    Desires
Chapter 37: Taking Responsibility for Yourself

Chapter 10: Understanding Your Own Thoughts, Feelings, and Desires

Former Secretary-General of the United Nations Kofi Annan said, "Knowledge is power. Information is liberating." Knowing your thoughts, feelings and desires is the first step in understanding them.

1. **Touch base with yourself. Frequently.** Just as we check in with people around us that we care about, it is important to check in with yourself as well. Knowing how you're feeling and doing can be very helpful in understanding where you are at and how you can move forward.

2. **Sit with your uncomfortable feelings.** Name them, honor them and recognize that they are also a part of your human experience. Acknowledging your own negative feelings can help you better understand yourself AND how to process them.

3. **Think about why you value what you do.** Take stock of your influences and experiences to know recognize your value system and the motivations and intentions that drive your actions.

4. **Recognize when maladaptive thinking negatively impacts your ability to make progress.** Sometimes our experiences give us skills that served us best in that instance, but not helpful in others. Self-awareness can be your best ally in such situations. Sometimes we get in our own way of progress, and recognizing when we are doing that can help us effectively move forward.

5. **Parse apart your desires and value systems.** Work on understanding what has influenced your desires and how your approach the world. Think about what you want from life versus what you might have been told you wanted based on societal or family expectations.

6. **Therapy can be helpful to understand motivations and thought patterns.** The process can help us staying attuned to our needs and feelings and developing more self-awareness.

7. **It is okay to have a totally unique value system!** Everyone has a unique and individual collection of experiences and influences in their life. It is unlikely that two people have the exact same value system, or that their values are constant throughout their lives. As we further our own experiences, we develop our own blend of what we place importance on in our lives.

8. **Self-awareness helpful to make progress in life toward goals.** Once you recognize what are your most valued desires and motivations, you can take effect steps to word towards your goals.

9. **Knowing what you need helps advocate for yourself.** Additionally, knowing where you might have limitations or might need additional support best aids you in reaching out for help as needed.

See also:
Chapter 4: Building a Support Team
Chapter 11: Online Support Groups
Chapter 37: Taking Responsibility for Yourself

Chapter 11: Online Support Groups

The Internet, for all its challenges, has ushered in new opportunities for support from professionals and strangers. The key is finding what works for you.

1. **In online support groups, people can share stories, experiences, and lives with others who have "been there."** Sharing with others can reduce isolation and loneliness by helping us see that there are others who are dealing with similar situations and who can help us get better.

2. **Support groups are open to anyone, but they are often focused on specific topics such as substance use, depression, family, divorce, or grief.** It may take time to find the right one for you and your current situation. Do not be discouraged if the first support group you find doesn't quite feel right. You should feel comfortable in the support group space that you choose, so trying different ones may help you determine the best fit.

3. **Twelve step groups are available 24/7 around the world.** Alcoholics Anonymous is the most well-known (for people who want to reduce or eliminate alcohol use), but there is also Al-Anon (for people with loved ones who are alcoholics), Narcotics Anonymous, Overeaters Anonymous, and other groups for specific challenges. Twelve step groups are anonymous and peer-led, run according to their principles that usually promote abstinence from substance use.

4. **Mental Health America has a comprehensive list of online support groups** for issues such as trauma/abuse, autism,

self-mutilation, overeating/eating disorders, depression, anxiety, and more at https://www.mhanational.org/find-support-groups.

5. **Generally, in self-help groups you will be asked to identify yourself by your first name only.** You are not required to tell your story the first time you go, and you can often just listen to others. You will be expected to keep what you hear confidential and to be respectful of others. You may also be invited to speak to others outside of the group or to obtain a sponsor, who is a person who looks out for you and guides you on your journey.

6. **There is wide variety of quality in online support groups.** If you're just starting out, it's good to stick to those that are moderated by a mental health professional or which are part of national/international traditions (such as twelve step groups), or which are recommended by reputable sources.

See also:
Chapter 4: Building a Support Team
Chapter 23: How to Express Yourself Without Alienating Others
Chapter 27: Processing Childhood Experiences

Chapter 12: Travel as Self-Exploration

In my (JPW) book, *Leaving Revolution: How We are Learning to Let Go and Move On*, I describe leaving for travel and adventure as one of the many ways we can learn about ourselves. Travel – whether an around-the-world trip or an afternoon at a park -- is an excellent opportunity for self-exploration.

1. **Travel gives us space to be and to think unfettered by the regular ebb and flow of life responsibilities, such as job, household management, friends, co-workers, or family.** This space is important for several reasons. First is the impact of just being in a space that is physically different from the usual habits of home, work, school, stores and so on. Have you ever been driving or taking the subway to work, and realize you've arrived after taking the correct turns automatically, without thinking about them? Adventuring puts you in a physically different space and has the impact of shaking out the well-worn pathways in your brain and forcing you to attend to your environment differently. It forces you to think and see differently.

2. **Traveling gives one *space to think*.** A nature trip gives plenty of space for solitude at natural vistas. In the big city, one can feel invisible walking down crowded streets. I know that not everyone leaves for adventure specifically to obtain space to think. Sometimes we leave for adventure with an intentional goal; for example, to heal from a breakup. But many times, it can be more amorphous. The topic that needs to be thought about might not be clear. The beauty of leaving for an adventure is that adventuring provides space to let the mind wander through memories, dreams, imaginative possibilities, and to work itself out.

3. **Travel also provides *space to be and grow*.** Paths in our daily life can wear grooves we don't even recognize that over time, close us in

and keep us tied to our habits. Similarly, our interactions with others (or our solitude) can create limitations that constrain us in ways we don't see until we've shaken up our routine. Adventuring can give space for us to act differently: to strike up a conversation with the stranger in the coffee shop in a way we never would at home or spend time with people we don't know.

4. **Travel doesn't have to be huge.** You don't have to wait until you can afford a plane trip to another country. You can go walk in a nearby park. You can take a day trip to somewhere you haven't been before. You can go away for a weekend by train or bus. Any small step you can take to get you out of your current routine can open doors for thinking and feeling differently.

5. **Bring a journal.** It might help to bring something to write on, just so you can make a note of whatever is on your mind. You never know what might come up!

6. **If you can't yet leave for travel, or if you just want to get started now, excellent** leaving for adventure stories include John Steinbeck's cross-country road trip *Travels with Charley in Search of America*, Cheryl Strayed's best-selling memoir *Wild*, detailing her trek up the Pacific Crest Trail, William Finnegan's *Barbarian Days* on his surfing adventure, and Elizabeth Gilbert's global journey, *Eat, Pray, Love*.

See also:

Chapter 13: Doing What You Love

When I (JW) was in training to become a psychologist, we had patients with depression identify positive events, no matter how small, and literally count the number of positive events they did each day to correlate it with their mood. This "pleasant events" list is a way to help you build positive emotions. Of course, this exercise also helps you to see how many little things are pleasant that you might not even identify. For me (SPK), I had a very varied and interesting path to get to where I am now. Growing up in India, it was hard to sometimes identify what it even was I loved doing. There were often societal and family expectations around what I should love, that influenced my work ethic and values. It's helpful to remember that you are allowed to change your mind, there's no set ways to do what you love.

1. **Make your own pleasant events list.** What are things you enjoy that bring you pleasure? Even small things, like looking out the window at the wind blowing through the trees, petting a cat, sorting vacation photos, or enjoying your favorite beverage. As you make your list, you will start to recognize how many things in your life bring you joy. You might also identify experiences you want to have or feelings you want to feel. Write those down too, and work toward achieving them.

2. **Look around where you live.** What do you like about where you live? Photos on the wall, books on the shelf, a plant that keeps living despite you always forgetting to water it, a comfy bed.

3. **If you're employed, what do you like about your job?** Some jobs stink, for sure. But if you're cleaning at a movie theater, maybe you get to see free movies? Or you meet nice people on the job? Or you have fun co-workers? Or maybe the only thing you like about your

job is the paycheck. Find something to appreciate, even if you decide you want to find a new job that's more enjoyable.

4. **Ask your friends what brings them joy.** Remember, even the little things can make you happy. And chatting with your friends about what you enjoy helps strengthen your relationship as well.

5. **Let the negative chatter go.** It's easy to get stuck, especially if you've been in a negative pattern for a while. You might think, "I enjoy hanging out with my friends," and then your mind goes into "… but I don't have a boyfriend/girlfriend. … And I don't see my friends that often. … and I don't know how much my friends really like me…" Stop that. Really. Just say "STOP" and go back to the positive. It's difficult. But it's worth it.

6. **Choose joy.** Some people are naturally happy and optimistic. The rest of us have to work at it. You can do this too. It may seem simple, but it feels a lot better to be happy than unhappy.

7. **Be thankful for what you have.** What is in your life that is good? Find gratitude for what is working, even if it's just a warm place to sleep, a pet that likes to snuggle, a college degree, or great hair. Practice gratitude.

8. **Set goals.** For anything that you don't like in your life, make a plan to get closer to what you want. Find a way to do what you love.

See also:
Chapter 1: Who Am I?
Chapter 3: Assessing Your Strengths
Chapter 19: Goal Setting

Chapter 14: Exercise

There's an old saying, "When your body is stuck, move your mind. When your mind is stuck, move your body." We have found this to be true, every single time.

1. **Physically, exercise is good for you in so many ways.** It gets your endorphins (feel good hormones) going, it improves your memory and brain function, helps lower blood pressure, improve heart health, improve sleep quality, reduce anxiety and depression, strengthens muscles and bones, boosts your immune system, reduces stress ... what's not to love?

2. **You don't have to run a marathon.** A walk around the block or up and down stairs can get your body moving enough to shift your mood. Of course, if you want to run a marathon, go for it!

3. **There are so many exercise options!** Walking and running are just the start. There are tons of online yoga and strength training classes. There are free training programs online that work with where you are to achieve any walking/running distance (I love the Couch to 5k programs!). There's tennis, pickleball, skiing, biking, summer softball, ultimate frisbee pick-up games, street hockey, ice hockey, roller skating ... so many choices!

4. **It's easy to be cost-conscious.** You just need a pair of shoes (which you already have) to go for a walk. Sometimes you can rent gear cheaply, buy used, or share with a friend. Classes at community centers sometimes provide gear for the duration of the class.

5. **Make it social.** Go for a walk or run with a friend. Join a running group. Meet up with a pal for a workout session. Train together for something. Challenge a buddy to a push up challenge in a month. So many options that can help you and your friends.

6. **Set some goals.** Since we're talking about moving your body, are there any goals you'd like to set? Maybe you want to lose weight, or be more social, or run a 5k, or improve your diet. Set some exercise-related goals and work toward reaching them.

7. **Make it a habit.** Meeting a pal weekly for an hour-long walk is a delightful habit to make. Or getting up just a bit earlier on the weekend to take the dog on an extra-long hike. It only takes a few weeks to make a habit.

8. **Overpower negative thoughts.** Some of us were raised to believe we weren't "fit" people, or "people who exercise" or whatever. Pffft! We can be who we choose to be in many areas, and exercise is one of them. Identify negative thoughts that tell you what you can't do and replace them with thoughts that tell you that you can.

9. **Work around injuries and limitations.** If you have a condition that makes it hard to run, you can likely still work out your upper body. If you have tennis elbow, you can still walk? Consult with your doctor and identify what you can do, then work on that.

10. **Help others.** There are walking, running, and biking events that include charity components. You can always decide to raise money for a charity while you're training for any event.

The support you'll get from friends, colleagues, and even strangers can be encouraging!

11. **Share with others and invite them to join you.** It's amazing how contagious enthusiasm can be. Sharing with others that you feel good walking or running or whatever can inspire them to make changes as well. Inviting others to go on a lunchtime walk with you is also positive for everyone. You can be the change you want to see.

See also:
Chapter 6: Thinking Long-Term
Chapter 17: Taking Stock of Your Influences
Chapter 39: Coming to Terms With Your Body

Chapter 15: Diet, Nutrition, and Sleep

Taking care of yourself means taking care of your whole body. In addition to regular medical, dental and mental health checkups, there are plenty of factors we can control at home. Diet, nutrition and sleep are vital in our holistic wellbeing.

1. **Take care of yourself.** We have just the one life and body. It is vital to do what is needed to take care of yourself to make life sustainable and stay healthy.

2. **Self-care can come in many forms.** Self-care looks different for different people. Reading, taking a walk, taking a bath, getting a massage, exercising, etc. are just a few different ways that people take care of themselves. They are vastly different, and all entirely valid ways!

3. **There are many different types of dietary options available.** Whether you eat meat, follow a vegetarian, vegan, low carbohydrate, or any other type of diet, ensure that you are getting all the nutrition you need. Mix and match if you like to make your dietary choice work for you.

4. **Avoid fad diets.** These can often be rooted in pseudoscience and can do more harm than good in the long run.

5. **Aim for sustainability.** Ultimately the best diet and exercise routines are the ones that you can maintain long term. Sustainability provides the most ongoing and lost lasting benefits.

6. **Approach it from the perspective of a lifestyle choice.** Incorporating your health choices into your day-to-day lifestyle can help make it more sustainable.

7. **Moderation is key.** As with anything, extreme choices whether they lean towards indulging or denying makes it harder to follow through. Moderation with both exercise and food choices allow you to enjoy them while still allowing for their health benefits.

8. **Guidelines are just that – guidelines.** Not a one size fits all, listen to your body's needs and adjust accordingly. You may hear personal well-meaning advice from lots of people around you; it doesn't mean the exact same thing will work for you!

9. **There can be both acute and chronic self-care activities.** Recognize what helps you with self-care in the moment and what are habits and copings skills that allow for long-term self-care on an ongoing basis.

10. **Any kind of diet, exercise and self-care can be tinkered with on an ongoing basis.** As situations and our bodies change, so do their needs. Be flexible in adjusting your routines to address your current needs.

See also:
Chapter 6: Thinking Long-Term
Chapter 37: Who to Surround Yourself With
Chapter 39: Coming to Terms With Your Body

Part III. Personal Identity and Belief Systems

Chapter 16: Gender Identity and Sexual Orientation

Many older folks are very confused about how young people talk about gender and sexual orientation. Even now, with the U.S. having come so far regarding diversity in gender identity and sexual orientation, it still can be challenging or intimidating to fully understand who we are and to share our identity with others.

1. **Let's break down the full LGBTQIAP+ acronym (often abbreviated to LGBTQ):**
   a. **Lesbian:** A woman physically, romantically, and/or emotionally attracted to other women.
   b. **Gay:** Gay people are those who are physically, romantically, and/or emotionally attracted to those of the same gender. It's used for both women and men. Some women prefer the word lesbian, and some refer to themselves as gay.
   c. **Bisexual:** People who are physically, romantically, and/or emotionally attracted to both men and women are called bisexual. It's often abbreviated to "bi."
   d. **Transgender:** Someone who identifies as a different gender than that of the body they were born in. Some use surgery and hormones to transition to the gender they're comfortable with though some don't need to do that. Note transgender is in the sexual orientation acronym, but it is a gender identity.
   e. **Queer/Questioning:** Queer is an umbrella term used by individuals who are not heterosexual and who may view other terms as too limiting. The term "Queer" was previously an insult that has been reclaimed by the community, so use it cautiously when referring to others. Questioning refers to individuals who are in the process

of understanding their sexual orientation or gender identity.

f. **Intersex:** An intersex person is someone who does not have distinct biological sex. It could be because of their reproductive organs, their chromosome patterns, or other reasons.

g. **Asexual:** A person who is asexual is someone who doesn't feel sexual desire. It varies from person to person as each person's sexuality is unique, but one should note that people who are asexual can have romantic or emotional attraction, can have a sex drive or sexual desire, and aren't necessarily celibate. They just have minimal to no sexual desire.

h. **Pansexual:** A pansexual is physically, emotionally, and/or romantically attracted to all people, no matter their sex or gender identity. This is different from bisexual as bisexuals are attracted to men and women, while pansexuals can be attracted to people who are intersex or nonbinary or anywhere on the gender spectrum.

i. **Plus:** The "plus" can include anyone who doesn't identify as any of the other letters; it can also just mean an intentional inclusivity.

2. **Note that sexual orientation is different from gender identity.** People can identify as any gender and have any sexual orientation in any combination. For example, a person who is transgender male to female (MTF) could be attracted to men, women, or others. It's generally not appropriate to assume or ask about sexual orientation unless you are specifically interested in dating or having sex with them.

3. **For many individuals older than 40 years old in the U.S., people who grew up in very conservative/religious families, and people in many parts of the world today,** coming out can

be a difficult process. Not only do we have societal expectations of our gender, when we get married (and to whom), who is appropriate to fall in love with, and how we should behave, we also have religion, nationality, and other parts of our identity that may also have their own perspectives on sexual orientation. In some parts of the world, homosexual sex is still against the law and can be punishable by death. In other cultures – including some in the U.S. – individuals who come out are shunned from their families, churches, or communities.

4. **Our beliefs about sexual orientation relate strongly to our beliefs about gender.** Some groups state that it's wrong to be LGBTQ; others state it's okay to *be* LGBTQ as long as you don't *act* on those urges (e.g., to engage in a loving relationship with someone to whom you're attracted). What are your beliefs about sexual orientation? Where do those beliefs come from? Have you heard people make positive or negative comments about individuals who were presumed gay? If you think it's not okay to be gay, what do you think people who are gay should do? If you believe being LGBTQ is a choice, do you think you could change your sexual orientation? Why or why not?

5. **Coming out (sharing who you are with others) is something you do when you are ready.** No one should pressure you into coming out, and you can share what you want with others only when you want to. If you want support working through who you are, it might be helpful to reach out to support groups online, such as PFLAG (Parents and Friends of Lesbians and Gays; they will help you) or your local Queer/LGBT Center. If you don't have a Center near you, reach out to one online or by phone and they will help you.

6. **There's no "right" way to be queer.** You don't have to use the words lesbian, gay, bisexual, or queer. You don't have to be sexually active. You don't have to dress a certain way or talk a certain way. You can just be you. Good LGBT support doesn't try to tell you how to be, talk, dress, or behave to be LGBT; they merely support you in your process of discovering who you are.

See also:

Chapter 17: Taking Stock of Your Influences

We do not grow up alone. From the time we are born, we are shaped by the different experiences and interactions we have with the people in our lives and our environment. My (SPK) love language is often food – it's a big part of my Indian upbringing!

1. **You can have many influences in life.** Family, friends, professional acquaintances are some of the people who can directly influence your life. Your cultural upbringing and your community can be broader influences in your day to day lives.

2. **There can be different influences for different aspects of life.** Everything in your life does not need to have a singular influence. The more exposure we receive during our experiences, the broader that influence can get.

3. **Identify your core values.** These are your guiding lights. They form the basis of how you develop your belief system.

4. **Know which value systems are constant and which can vary depending on situation.** Knowing your core values help guide which parts of your belief systems are fluid based on the context you are in.

5. **You can pick parts of different value systems.** Your belief system does not need to neatly fall into a pre-determined box. You can tailor your own by recognizing what is important to you. Self-awareness and awareness of the situation and people you are interacting with can help you highlight and choose what strategies will best serve in that instance.

6. **Taking stock of your influences is a fluid, interactive process.** Ongoing life experiences keep adding to your perspective.

7. **Address what no longer serves you best.** Sometimes the influences we have in our life are not positive and do not help with personal growth. When something no longer is serving your best interests, acknowledge that and make the changes needed to move forward.

8. **Nurture relationships that help you grow.** Work on developing those relationships in life that help your personal growth and move towards your hopes and goals. Recognize what relationships bring positive value in your life and foster those.

9. **Be honest with yourself.** Touching base with yourself and knowing what influences your motivations, desires, and actions will allow you to take an honest stock of where you stand and where to go from here.

See also:
Chapter 4: Building a Support Team
Chapter 27: Processing Childhood Experiences
Chapter 37: Who to Surround Yourself With

Chapter 18: Religion and Spiritual Beliefs

Many of us were raised in a religious environment, and nearly all of us are aware of various religions that exist in the world. In addition, we might also be aware that being religious and being spiritual can be two totally different things. What do you believe? Read on…

1. **There are a variety of belief systems in the world.** Whether they are guided by religion, culture or geography there is a myriad of different beliefs that people and communities hold.

2. **Religion is a collection of cultural systems, belief systems, and worldviews that relate to spirituality and, sometimes, to moral values.** Most religions have narratives, symbols, traditions, and sacred histories intended to give meaning to life or to explain the origin of life or the universe. These beliefs and traditions may also guide our behavior by indicating what is or is not acceptable behavior within our community.

3. **Spiritual beliefs generally address an existential perspective on life, death, and the nature of reality.** Spiritual beliefs may include the relationship to a superior being, and like religion, may provide guidelines for how we behave.

4. **Specific practices can be spiritual, religious or both.** These include:
    a. **Prayer.** Prayer is the practice of speaking to the superior being, nature, spirits, or energy of your own understanding. Many times, prayer can help people feel connected to the spiritual being/universe around them.

    b. **Gratitude** is often a part of prayer. Depending on your beliefs, you may thank the superior being for the world, experiences, their beneficence, or anything else.

    c. **Group services.** People who believe similarly may gather for religious or spiritual services. These could include group Christian, Muslim, or Jewish services in a house of worship, or a Wiccan or shaman gathering, or many other ways of expressing beliefs together.

    d. **Holy texts.** We're familiar with the Christian Bible, the Jewish Torah, and the Muslim Qu'ran. Many religions and some spiritual belief systems have texts that exist to guide believers. Some people believe in the texts literally, whereas others use them more generally as stories to interpret.

5. **There are significant differences among spiritual and religious practices.**

    a. **Monotheism, polytheism, or atheism.** Different traditions believe in one God (monotheism; Christianity, Judaism, Islam), more than one god (polytheism; Hindu, Hare Krishna, paganism), or no god (atheism; Buddhism, Shintoism, Satanism). Some spiritual traditions such as shamanism believe in the existence of spirits or other energy in the world; still others, such as Unitarian-Universalism, are open about what adherents believe and welcome everyone.

    b. **Origin story.** Many religions and spiritual beliefs have a perspective on how the world or humanity began. From Christianity's Adam and Eve story to Hindus' belief that Brahma created the universe out of himself, these beliefs have helped humans find a way to understand why we are here.

    c. **Funeral rites.** Many groups have specific rituals associated with death, including burying/not burying, cremating/not cremating, specific practices for bathing the body, and words to say over the body.

d. **After death beliefs.** Most religions have a perspective on what happens after we die, whether that includes going to heaven/hell/purgatory, being reincarnated, or something else.

e. **Rituals.** Rituals such as prayers, baptism, marriage rites, communion, confession, meditation, yoga, chanting, performing charitable acts, and others can be embedded into religious traditions or created as desired.

6. **If you're not sure what you want, go exploring.** Regardless of where you are related to your own beliefs, it's often fun and fascinating to learn more. Ask your friends about their experiences with religion. If they were raised differently than you, ask even more questions about their beliefs and what they like and don't like about their religion. You may want to try visiting different houses of worship, reading books on different religions, or even taking a class on comparative religion to learn more about what is out there. There's no harm in exploring, and it will help you better understand what you truly believe.

7. **Consider the role your family, heritage, and upbringing play in your beliefs.** Cultural influences can be very strong. The community someone grew up in, their family structure and their larger cultural background can have a huge influence on how their belief and value system develops. It is important and helpful to keep that in mind when identifying your motivations and guiding your interactions with others.

8. **It's helpful to view different systems as just that – different.** Different influences and perspectives make belief systems not

independently right or wrong, the context they are in matters a lot. It is a different perspective, driven by different values.

9. **Identify values that sit right with your conscience.** Although beliefs may not be right or wrong on their own, they may be right or wrong for you. Knowing what is important to you will help you nurture values that align with your core values.

10. **Respect other beliefs and motivations.** We do not know what experiences or influences have contributed to someone else's belief system. Recognize and respect that different people bring a variety of perspectives based on their influences.

11. **Consider what you would like to experience now.** Think about what would happen if you let go of others' expectations and wishes for you, just for a moment. If you could choose what you want in your life regarding religious and spiritual beliefs, what would that look like? How you were raised will always be a part of your heritage and your background. As an adult, you can make decisions about how you want to live, including your religious beliefs.

12. **You can believe anything you want; you might as well believe what makes you happy.** Seriously. Life is short.

See also:

Part IV. Life Changes

Chapter 19: Goal Setting

You have lots of ideas of what you'd like to accomplish, but somehow, you still fall behind. *You are not alone.* Goal setting is a skill -- and it's not one we tend to learn in school! Many times, people get caught up striving for perfection, and this keeps them stuck. It's important to remember that the point is to meet your goals, not have them be "perfect".

1. **Identify the overall content areas that you wish to address.** This could include career; finance; education; relationship; physical/health; emotional/mental health; attitude/perspective. Goals aligned with your core values are easier to stick with. It's also helpful to articulate the "why" behind your goal so when it gets hard you can remind yourself. Write them down!

2. **Set goals that you want to achieve.** This is vital, since we let our goal setting often be determined by "shoulds," rather than "wants" or "needs." Brainstorm what feels important to you, differentiating this from any "shoulds" or external expectations.

3. **Now break down your list into component,** or sub-goals. For example, if you want to go back to school, sub-goals might include looking for available programs; determining the admission criteria; assessing financial aid; determining a plan for time management, etc. There are likely many more steps, and these sub-goals often can be broken down even further. Follow the SMART acronym to define your goals. Ensure your goals are: Specific, Measurable, Action Oriented, Realistic, and Time-Based.

4. **Pick ONE goal to start working on.** Too often people try to address multiple goals at the same time, which takes longer, and dilutes the process. Write down your goal, in SMART format and put it in several visible and accessible places (bathroom mirror, door of the fridge, inside of your planner).

5. **Estimate the time needed to reach each step of your goal.** If you're not sure, ask someone with experience in that area for their opinion.

6. **Plan and schedule time in your day to address your goal.** Don't wait until you're "in the mood" (that's one of the main reason people fall off in progress). Start with small goals and short time frames. Using the example above, you might schedule (2) 15-minute times during the week when you will research doctoral programs.

7. **State each goal as a positive statement** (what you will do, not what you "won't" do).

8. **Have a contingency plan.** There's a great phrase "no plan survives first contact" which means that it's important to recognize the ways in which problems may arise and have a general outline on an alternative so you can adapt and keep moving forward.

9. **If you achieved the goal easily,** make your next goal a little harder. Similarly, if it took a long time to meet your goal, make sure your next goal a little easier or break your goals into smaller steps – you are working to build on success.

10. **If a goal is too big then it can seem like you're not making progress.** If this happens, clarify your sub-goals that will help

you reach your big goal. Keeping these sub-goals small and incremental gives you greater rewards.

11. **Create a daily "to-do" list – and keep it manageable!** Overcommitting is another procrastination trap.

12. **Identify and celebrate the small steps** you made in the right direction even if you didn't reach the final goal. Believe in the process – imagine that each one of the steps towards your goal is a Lego block. It takes a lot of tiny blocks to make a structure.

13. **If you run into an obstacle,** ask your support system for help in identifying a solution or offering a different perspective.

14. **Keep in mind that if you do not reach your goal this does not make you a failure.** It's a process, so analyze which of the SMART steps needs adjustment. Ask yourself what you learned from the experience that might help you in achieving future goals. Adapting your expectations and priorities is part of the growth process. While we may not achieve every goal exactly as we imagined, we always can learn and move forward, even if it's in a new direction.

15. **Celebrate your achievements and be proud of your accomplishments!**

See also:
Chapter 3: Assessing Your Strengths
Chapter 6: Thinking Long-Term
Chapter 13: Doing What You Love

Chapter 20: Choosing or Changing Careers

How did you choose a career? Some of us have known what we want to be since we were little; others are still trying to figure it out.

1. **What does having a career mean to you?** For some people it's essential to have the identity as an accountant or banker or teacher or barista. For others, what they do for work is just a way to make some money so they can afford to do the things they really want to do. Is a "career" important to you? If so, why?

2. **There are so many options for careers!** The U.S. Bureau of Labor Statistics has occupation profiles that list every major occupation in the country, including the number of people in the occupation, estimated wages, training/experience required, related industries, and employment outlook. It doesn't include brand new occupations, like social media influencer, that are still emerging. Just search online.

3. **College provides only moderate preparation for real-life, and college isn't even required.** There is a hearty debate about the value of college in preparing individuals for real (adult) life. Certainly, there's value inherent in learning how to think and in developing a broad spectrum of understanding humanities, literature, and other topics. That said, college isn't for everyone, and many jobs don't require college at all.

4. **Do you want to change your job or change your career?** Sometimes we like what we're doing for work, just not the people we're doing it with (or for). Other times, we want to do something totally different. Consider what you like and don't like about your job. This could be issues like the salary,

benefits, hours, work conditions, colleagues, customers, product, bosses, impact on social issues, or something else. If you're not sure, every day for a week, write down 3 things you enjoyed/liked and 3 things you didn't enjoy/like. It will become clear!

5. **Generation Z and Millennials are changing jobs and careers much more quickly than Generation X and Baby Boomers.** Our parents' generation cautioned us against job hopping and urged us to stick with one job. Many of us saw our parents miserable at work, or laid off, or unfulfilled. The world has changed significantly, and it's okay to move around if we want. Consider your long-term goals, obligations, and responsibilities, and have at it!

6. **Update your resume or CV.** Regardless of how you may or may not immediately use your resume, updating it will remind you of your value, experiences, and interests. It will also make you more prepared no matter what you choose.

7. **Informational interviews can be enormously helpful in learning about options.** Identify people in careers or industries you're interested in through word of mouth or through LinkedIn and reach out to them for an informational interview. Ask for 20 minutes of their time and prepare questions such as, How did you get into this role? What do you like about your job? What do you not like? What advice do you have? Be sure to thank them, in writing if possible.

8. **Career choices are not always rational or logical decisions.** Keeping your eyes and ears open, talking with people about what you're looking for (such as, "I'm just starting to think about what else might be out there, career-wise") and

intentionally noticing what kinds of work people are doing will help you move in the right direction.

9. **There are also surveys available online** that can help you identify the kinds of careers you might be interested in based on your interests and skills. Search online for "career interest inventory."

10. **Remember you are responsible for your career, and life is long.** You will figure this out – or not. It's fun to experience wherever your path takes you.

See also:
Chapter 3: Assessing Your Strengths
Chapter 6: Thinking Long-Term
Chapter 13: Doing What You Love

Chapter 21: Continuing Education and Professional Training

Regardless of where you are in your career or job search, many of us want to keep learning. Both of us are lifelong learners, and we hope you are too! Here are some ideas for how to keep learning even after you finish initial school or training.

1. **Many employers provide free training.** This can include content training (accounting, therapy), program training (spreadsheets, programming), or soft skills training (communication, conflict management). Check out what might be available.

2. **Some organizations provide an annual or quarterly stipend or funds for external training.** Others don't pay for training but will allow you to attend on work time without having to take time off. It's worth investigating.

3. **Tuition reimbursement is awesome.** Larger organizations might provide tuition reimbursement to work toward a degree program or certification program. Some require the training to be in your direct field; others will support any programs.

4. **Independent study.** There are plenty of resources online and books at the library or bookstore to learn about new topics such as project management, veterinary science, or auto mechanic. If you want to learn something new, there are literally tons of resources.

5. **If you want to improve soft skills, you can ask your boss for additional tasks or increasing responsibility.** They might be able to delegate a project or part of project to you, which could help you improve your skills at leading, managing, organizing, and communicating.

6. **You can ask to report to others on something you learned.** This will involve you doing the research, preparing a presentation, getting feedback, and speaking publicly to your small (or large) team.

7. **Talk to an expert.** If there's something you really want to know, do your homework first, then call up someone who can explain it to you. You'd be surprised how many people are eager to share their expertise with you, especially if you're prepared. Have your questions ready.

8. **Learn as a group.** You can invite friends or colleagues with similar interests to learn together. Identify a book or an article you can read independently and discuss together.

9. **State and federal governments have resources.** Search for federal or state + topic. There are resources including books, booklets, pamphlets, and trainings, many of which are free, on just about any topic.

10. **Check out professional organizations.** Whatever your field, there is a professional association, guild, or society. Check it out online first. Then consider if you want to take advantage of the resources posted online, join as a member, reach out to members to discuss your interests, or attend an annual meeting or training.

See also:
Chapter 3: Assessing Your Strengths
Chapter 6. Thinking Long-Term
Chapter 22. Should I Move Around Or Settle Down?

Chapter 22: Should I Move Around Or Settle Down

"Should I stay, or should I go?" is, for many of us, a lifelong question. In my (JPW) book, *Leaving Revolution: How We are Learning to Let Go and Move On*, I describe "stayers" and "leavers," and indicate we can be stayers and leavers in different parts of our lives.

1. **What kind of life do you want?** This is really the important question in all aspects of getting your shit together. If you want the kind of life where you go to the coffee shop at the corner and they know your name, you enjoy staying and growing in the same company over time, you like seeing the neighborhood kids grow up (maybe with yours?), and you feel safe and comfy in your home, you might be a stayer. If, on the other hand, you love the sense of adventure with moving around, you love exploring new things, you can't imagine staying at the same job for ten years, and you love looking for new places and neighborhoods to live, you might be a leaver. Of course, many of us are somewhere in the middle of those two extremes.

2. **Costs of staying vs. going.** There are financial costs to moving homes, for example, but there are also fewer tangible costs of staying. "Opportunity cost" is the term for what you're missing out on by choosing the path you did. Moving includes costs of a moving truck, deposits, and your time to pack, but sometimes not moving means you're unhappy somewhere you don't want to be. There are always opportunity costs. There is always the path not taken. We all do the best we can with the information we have, and we keep forging forward.

3. **Consider what you're looking for.** This is somewhat different from "what kind of life do you want?" If you're thinking of changing something or leaving, what are you hoping will be different? Maybe you'll feel freer, or more secure, or less scattered. Maybe you want to be a fish out of water and you're tired of the same old thing. Knowing what you are hoping to change will help you decide how to move forward. Sometimes there is a way to achieve what you're looking for without moving homes or changing jobs. Perhaps that's a reasonable choice?

4. **Take it step by step.** Sometimes we don't plan to be leavers or stayers, but over time our decisions accumulate into patterns. That's okay. Make each decision as best you can, and all will become clear.

See also:
Chapter 3: Assessing Your Strengths
Chapter 6: Thinking Long-Term
Chapter 20: Choosing or Changing Careers

Part V. Social Situations and Community Building

Chapter 23: How to Express Yourself Without Alienating Others

How we interact with the world guides how we fit into it. Communication, both verbal and non-verbal, is important and is a two-way street. How we communicate with others influences how others communicate with us.

1. **Be honest but not rude.** Honesty is important to effective communication. You can be truthful without being mean or rude about it.

2. **Be empathetic.** Do your best to understand where the other person is coming from in a conversation.

3. **Show kindness and compassion.** Having a conversation in a kind and respectful manner will go far in achieving a common goal.

4. **Have an idea of what you want to say before you enter the conversation.** What are you trying to communicate? What is the point of the communication? Knowing the answers to those questions will help you have the conversation more effectively.

5. **Write down what you need to say.** Having your points laid out on paper might help you stay on track and refocus on the objective of the communication.

6. **Identify your personal motivations.** Knowing if you are trying to communicate something that requires follow up or if you are just looking to vent without any input from the other person can help you prep the other person for

what to expect. Let them know beforehand if you want or do not want their input.

7. **Run it by someone else if you're unsure of how it will be received.** If you're not sure if what you're trying to say might be rude or disrespectful to the other person, run it by something who can provide you with an objective perspective.

8. **Know the relationship and its boundaries.** Recognize what topics of conversation might be touchy subjects for people, and if you know their boundaries – respect them.

9. **Be mindful of the setting.** Know the limits and "norms" of appropriateness of conversational topics in settings. For example – often polarizing or deeply personal topics such as religion or politics are often frowned upon in professional settings.

10. **Clearly communicate your own boundaries.** If you have conversational triggers or a preferred communication style, let the other person know that. It can only help with more effective conversations.

11. **It is okay make mistakes.** We are not perfect and should not expect to have every conversation perfectly. It is human to make mistakes when we don't have all the necessary knowledge.

12. **Hold yourself accountable when you err.** Although it is human to make mistakes, holding yourself accountable and not repeating mistakes can help maintain relationships.

13. **Agree to disagree.** Somethings you cannot find common ground – that is okay. Respectfully agreeing to disagree is an effective communication method that acknowledges individuality.

See also:

Chapter 10: Understanding Your Own Thoughts, Feelings, and Desires

Chapter 34: Being Kind to Others

Chapter 35: What to Share With Family, Friends, and Co-Workers

Chapter 24: Avoiding Cults and People Who Will Take Advantage of You

Our mothers warned us that there were bad people in the world, but as kids, it was hard to believe. As grown-ups, though, we may have had experiences where we see that there are people who are not nice or who want to take advantage of us, gaslight us, or worse. Here's how to keep those antennae up to stay safe.

1. **Listen with curiosity.** Sometimes it takes people a while to relax and open up, so unless all the alarms are going off, allow a little time to assess.

2. **While you're listening with curiosity, pay attention to what you're seeing.** Body language can help you understand the meaning behind their words. How they dress or groom themselves can be important. Posture tells you whether someone is potentially too aggressive (taking up all the space), defensive (folded in on themselves) or just not interested (turned away and avoiding eye contact). Pay attention to their facial expressions. How are they using their body? Are they taking up too much space or do you feel uncomfortable by their frequent touching or large body moments? If they avoid eye contact, or their smile doesn't seem genuine, that's a red flag. Are they checking out other people while you're together or seeing who else is in the room? Do they sound overly critical or negative, or super sweet and insincere? Are they too perfect?

3. **Also notice how you feel.** Flattery and validation feel good but check for feelings of substance. If you feel enriched by

the interaction, that's a great sign. If they've shaken your hand or hugged you and want to wipe your hand off or back away, this is a big red flag. What is your gut instinct telling you? If your mind says, "They're great", but your gut says something is off – pay attention!

4. **Be judicious with your time.** You are under no obligation to continue a conversation if you're getting creeped out or even if you just don't want to. You can almost always just say "Excuse me, I need to go," and leave. If anyone gives you a hard time when you try to leave, that's confirming you are making the right decision to walk away.

5. **Be aware of gaslighting.** Gaslighting is a form of emotional manipulation in which the abuser attempts to sow self-doubt and confusion in their victim's mind by distorting reality and forcing the recipient to question their own judgment and intuition. If you feel confused and upset after a conversation, and especially if you find you're always wrong when you talk with someone, they may be gaslighting you.

6. **Cults are groups of people who follow a similar ideology, usually led by a charismatic leader.** Many, but not all, cults can be dangerous, mind-controlling, and potentially violent. It's best to identify and stay away from cults to begin with by being careful about groups you join. If you are asked to join a group, research them online. Be wary of groups that have a charismatic leader, are suspicious of outsiders, have strict rules, try to isolate you from your family and friends, try to love bomb you, or ask for money. Ask lots of questions and push back if they try to control you or change your beliefs.

7. **Talk to people you trust about these kinds of experiences.** Friends or family members you trust can provide a different perspective on what you're experiencing and help you make sense of it. You can also talk with a therapist.

See also:
Chapter 3: Assessing Your Strengths
Chapter 18: Religion and Spiritual Beliefs
Chapter 37: Who to Surround Yourself With

Chapter 25: Making Sense of the World Around You

Politics have become a leading area of divisiveness in the U.S. It seems like lawmakers no longer "reach across the aisle," and disinformation has become rampant. How to make sense of politics, the environment, and this very weird reality we are in?

1. **Examine where you're getting your news.** There are many sources online that indicate whether news outlets are conservative, liberal, or any place in between. If you're confused by what you're hearing, find news sources that are generally in the middle between liberal and conservative.

2. **What is important to you?** The list of "political" issues is long: abortion, the environment, the economy, national security, voting rights, worker safety, inequality, homelessness, human rights. You may have very strong opinions about some, and not know much about others. If you're not sure, you don't have to take on every issue at once. Start with one thing that's interesting to you, and start reading about it, listening to podcasts about it, and talking with others about it. The more you can learn about different issues, the more you can determine what is important to you.

3. **Think critically about what you're hearing.** Sadly, not everyone communicates in ways that are direct, honest, or even consistent. Sometimes what people are advocating depends on who is paying them! To think critically, consider the source of information, including who is paying them, what they've advocated for in the past, and whom might be benefiting from what they are advocating.

Consider alternative explanations. Consider how different kinds of people (especially those different from them) would be affected by what they're advocating. Think about what assumptions they or you might be making.

4. **Pay attention to body language.** If newscasters, reporters, or politicians look angry or smug or calm or confident what does that say about them? Sometimes people look angry because they are passionate about a topic, and other times they are intentionally trying to rile people up. A few politicians have been found to exaggerate their accents to make them seem more likeable by people in their area. What does body language tell you about the person you're hearing?

5. **Be suspicious of habits.** Some of us grew up with families that "always vote Democrat" or "have always been Republican." That's perfectly fine for them. It's also okay for you to do your own homework and figure out what is important to you. You don't have to tell anyone who you vote for.

6. **What is your reality?** Politicians often say what they are experiencing or what will get people to vote for them. Politicians can say prices are going up, but what are you seeing at the gas pump or in the grocery store? Politicians can say crime is up or down, but what do the statistics for your neighborhood show? It can be confusing and frustrating to hear people saying things that are not consistent with your reality. The good part is, you have your own experience, and you can always compare what they are saying to what you are experiencing.

7. **Vote.** Part of being a responsible citizen is engaging in one of our most important rights, the right to vote for what is important to us. Register to vote (just look online for your state's process), do your homework, and vote for what is important to you.

See also:
Chapter 6: Thinking Long-Term
Chapter 17: Taking Stock of Your Influences
Chapter 43: Taking Responsibility for Yourself

Chapter 26: Building a Better World Through Diversity, Equity, and Inclusion

In *Millennials' Guide to Diversity, Equity, and Inclusion,* Lisa D. Jenkins and I (JPW) talk about how to use your experiences of diversity, equity, and inclusion to make the world a better place. Let's get started!

1. **Cultural diversity can be defined as an acceptance and acknowledgement of individuals coming from different cultures, races, or ethnicities.** Embracing cultural diversity includes respecting individual differences, acknowledging and celebrating these differences. It allows diverse groups to feel empowered to be seen and heard whether in their workplace, education setting, daily life, and within society. You can also consider diversity in occupation, skills and abilities, personality traits, and values. People embody many different aspects—from the obvious (e.g., race) to the not-so-obvious (e.g., political views) – of diversity.

2. **Diverse communities and workplaces have the advantage of a synergy of the varied ideas and experiences from different people who bring new and fresh ideas to the table.** Diverse people bring different perspectives. As a result, your team gains creativity and innovation. If you have a group of people representing four generations, with different countries of origin, representing various socio-economic sectors, you are bound to have a wide range of ideas and viewpoints which offer great value. The key is an environment that encourages a respectful and healthy dialogue of questions, thoughts and recommendations with the purpose of moving the company bottom line.

3. **Equity takes into consideration that diversity factors (e.g., race, gender) affect our status, rights, freedoms, and access to resources.** Equity provides disadvantaged individuals what they need so they can succeed, even if this means some people get more resources than others. For example, equality is when a teacher gives each child one apple; equity is when the teacher gives more food to those who are hungry and less food to those who brought their own lunch, so that all children are fed.

4. **Inclusion is an effort and practice to ensure that people who have different backgrounds are culturally and socially accepted, welcomed, and treated equally.** Inclusion goes beyond "tolerance" of diversity and ensuring an equitable workplace; it calls for actively embracing differences, empowering the inherent worth and dignity of all people, and ensuring everyone is welcome.

5. **To make the world a better place, start with being mindful.** Mindfulness means being conscious and aware of the cultural norms and cues in your organization and how those cultural norms and cues affect the mission of the company and your success as an employee. It's up to you to take inventory of your environment as well as your own values, beliefs and how you perceive others.

6. **Make the world a better place by being an ally or advocate.** Being an ally is being a collaborator who fights injustice and promotes equity through supportive personal relationships and acts of advocacy. Being an advocate goes even further and actively solicits others to join the cause, increase awareness, and engage hearts and minds. Don't rely on people from underrepresented groups to educate you, as that's an unfair burden on them. Do your own homework.

7. **Make the world better by building belonging.** Advocate for others who are different or who may feel marginalized because of their identity. It's easy to be silent, but it's much more challenging and advantageous to suggest that the hijab that your neighbor or co-worker wears is not a disturbance or distraction as some may claim. You can speak up and let others know how important it is that she is comfortable in her attire so that she can feel like she belongs. Everybody wins.

8. **Make the world better by building bridges.** Partner with someone who is different with the intention of facilitating positive and diverse change in your community or company. The two of you can become ambassadors and build bridges of inclusion. Know that when you build bridges of inclusion, you're building bridges of opportunities. These opportunities are not just for others, but when you become a bridge builder, you will find that you are stretched to know more and to do more. It's a win-win situation!

See also:
Chapter 16: Gender Identity and Sexual Orientation
Chapter 34: Being Kind to Others
Chapter 37: Who to Surround Yourself With

Part VI. Personal Situations

Chapter 27: Processing Childhood Experiences

Formative experiences are incredibly important in shaping our world views and how we interact with our environment throughout our lives. Whether these are positive childhood experiences, such as secure family dynamics and pleasant memories, or adverse experiences, such as abuse or neglect, they play a major role in how we see ourselves and how we move forward in life.

1. **Our perspective can be skewed.** It is hard to get a complete picture when you have been in the thick of any experience. Connecting with other people involved in those experiences can help broaden our understanding.

2. **They can help understand our value system.** Since formative experiences are so ingrained in our development, understanding those influences can help you understand your own value system.

3. **They can provide insight into motivations and coping skills.** As childhood experiences help develop our value system, they also can help providing insight into what drives you and how you approach different situations.

4. **Our body remembers how we felt.** Even if we don't consciously remember how we felt in different situations, our body systems remember the different emotions associated with them. We can have instinctive reactions based on our body's memories. When I (SPK) read the "The Body Keeps the Score by Bessel van der Kolk", I was

amazed at the sheer number of ways our body processed traumatic experiences.

5. **Getting a better understanding of these helps make more informed choices about future decisions.** Knowing our motivations and behaviors, and the reasons for those can help guide how we move forward in working towards our goals.

6. **Processing them can give us enough understanding.** Understanding allows us to actively make different choices.

7. **Processing traumatic experiences can be uncomfortable.** That is normal and human. Processing trauma helps us integrate our experiences in a meaningful way in our lives.

8. **Therapy can be helpful to process the trauma in a safe space.** Therapists are trained to help guide the process of recognizing, understanding and making sense of trauma from our childhood. They are also trained to help you work on developing skills to cope with it in a healthy way.

9. **Explore support groups for other adults with similar childhood experiences.** This can be validating and help you feel less alone.

See also:
Chapter 4: Building a Support Team
Chapter 6: Thinking Long-Term
Chapter 33: When Situations Seem to Repeat Themselves

Chapter 28: Family Expectations of You

Just as we don't grow up in a vacuum, we generally don't live our lives in one either. Family interactions often make up a big part of the day-to-day interactions we have with our world. It is a human experience for family to express and pass on their expectations of us. This is particularly common in many collectivist cultures where the importance is placed more on family cohesion and group dynamics than individual preferences.

1. **Family expectations can create a lot of pressure.** There can be a lot of guilt associated with not living up to those expectations. Recognize what is reasonable and achievable for you.

2. **They can conflict with your own desires.** Sometimes your family will expect you to do the opposite of what you want to do. Remember that you are good enough just the way you are.

3. **If your parent's expectations conflict with your/their value system,** communicate that to them respectfully.

4. **You can decide** how much you want those expectations to influence your life choices.

5. **What do you value more?** Is it your relationship with family members or doing what you want?

6. **Recognize that your family members are also human.** They are also just people with their own desires, motivations, and hope.

7. **Connect with someone you trust** to get an objective perspective.

8. **See if there can there be a compromise.** Depending on your values, there may be a middle ground in moving forward.

9. **Focus on shared goals.** There may be some common elements in your family expectations and your own desires.

10. **If you feel like you've reached an impasse,** you can agree to disagree and move to other safe topics of conversation.

11. **Ultimately recognize that you must live with the choices that are made.** This includes whatever follows that.

12. **Reaffirm your choices by checking in with yourself.** Does this way forward still align with my values? You are allowed to change your mind and your path – this does not have to mean you made a mistake!

See also:

Chapter 29: Family and Religion

Many of us were raised in our family's religion. For some of us, it remains a meaningful part of our everyday life, a way to connect with our family, and a part of who we are. For others of us, our family's religion is not something we relate to anymore, and it is not a source of comfort. So, what do you do now?

1. **Reflect on your family's religious and spiritual beliefs.** Think back to how you were raised. Did you go to a house of worship regularly? Did you read spiritual books together as a family or pray together? What were the positive parts of those experiences for you? Were there negative aspects of those experiences?

2. **Go exploring.** Regardless of where you are related to your own beliefs, it's often fun and fascinating to learn more. Ask your friends about their experiences with religion. If they were raised differently than you, ask even more questions about their beliefs and what they like and don't like about their religion. You may want to try visiting different houses of worship, reading books on different religions, or even taking a class on comparative religion to learn more about what is out there. There's no harm in exploring, and it will help you better understand what you truly believe.

3. **Consider what is non-negotiable vs. what is flexible for you.** Some people have cultural identities or jobs tied into their religious beliefs. You may be certain you believe in one God but also not be certain that you are Protestant or Catholic or Jewish or Muslim. Similarly, you might be

certain you are Christian, but interested in exploring other denominations. Make that part of your exploration!

4. **What do you want to feel from your religion?** Many people describe that they want their religious identity and actions to make them feel safe, secure, and like they belong. Others feel they need religious dictates to help keep them on the "straight and narrow." Still others may have never thought about it at all. Understanding what you want to experience can help you think through what you're looking for.

5. **Take a break – or step it up?** Maybe it would be useful to take a break from regular services or activities so you can see how you feel when you don't have those activities in your life regularly. Or maybe you want to accelerate your experience, and go to services more frequently, take classes at your house of worship, or engage in additional reading? Whatever route you choose, see how you feel to help guide you.

6. **What might consequences be if you made a shift?** Sometimes people are worried about sharing their questions with others in their family or friend circle, because they are worried about how they might be viewed. Some religions welcome questioning and doubt; others do not accept it. Consider what might happen if you started talking with people you're close to about how you're feeling. You don't have to talk with them now; you can continue to learn on your own. That said, if you're feeling you might be punished or shunned for raising doubts, that's also good information to have.

7. **Consider what you would like to experience now.** Think about what would happen if you let go of your parents'

expectations and wishes for you, just for a moment. If you could choose what you want in your life regarding religious and spiritual beliefs, what would that look like? How you were raised will always be a part of your heritage and your background. As an adult, you can make decisions about how you want to live, including your religious beliefs.

See also:
Chapter 1: Who Am I?
Chapter 27: Processing Childhood Experiences
Chapter 28: Family Expectations of You

Chapter 30: Violence, Sexual Assault, and Rape

Violence is an unfortunate and ugly reality. Human history and sadly, human nature has shown many instances of treating other humans as subpar and inflicting violence and trauma.

1. **A gentle affirmation: No assault is your fault.**

2. **You are not responsible for the choices made by the perpetrator** and the blame lies solely with the assaulter.

3. **Do whatever is needed to keep yourself safe in the moment.** Trust your instincts in that situation.

4. **Seek help to process the complex feelings that are associated with it.** Therapy can be helpful in working through the trauma.

5. **The RAINN Hotline: 800-656-HOPE (4673)** is the nation's largest anti-sexual violence organization. They offer crisis support through both chat and phone at any time.

6. **Getting medical care, an ER visit or getting a rape kit done.** Choosing any medical care after a sexual assault is a deeply personal decision. If you want to document and treat injuries, get emergency contraception, or receive preventative medicine for sexually transmitted infections (STIs) you can go to the doctor of your choice or an emergency room (ER) for these services.

7. **If staying by yourself after feels unsafe, reach out to your support group.** Stay with friends or family if company is helpful.

8. **Remember that you are not obligated to do anything (report) if you are not comfortable with it.** Although, there can be a lot of guilt associated with reporting or not reporting, either choice is okay, and a trusted friend or therapist can help affirm your choices.

9. **Explore survivor's support groups in your community.** Hearing other's survival stories can make you feel less alone and isolated in the experience.

See also:
Chapter 3: Assessing Your Strengths
Chapter 4: Building a Support Team
Chapter 5: Emergencies

Chapter 31: Parental Struggles

Because of the intimate connection we have with our parents, it can be difficult to separate who they are from who we are. This includes their successes, failures, expectations, personality flaws. When their health wavers such as with mental illness or substance use issues or they are there too much (helicopter parents) or not enough (absentee parents), it can shape the early parts of our path, but it is up to us where to go from there.

1. **Identify what your needs are.** Determine what you really need from your interactions with your parents.

2. **Identify what your values are.** Your interactions outside of those with your family may lead to you developing a value system that is different from the one your parents might have – that is okay!

3. **Practice acceptance.** This doesn't mean making a value judgement on whether the situation or dynamic is right or wrong, it means accepting what is beyond your control and focusing on finding a path forward within what you do have control over.

4. **You can't change them, but you can change your relationship with them.** You have the power to break the cycle and change the dynamic you share with them.

5. **Work on finding common ground.** When we have a tense relationship with our parents it can be easy to focus on the sources of conflict.

6. **Recognize that your parents are also human.** As much as we like to think of our parents as invincible and unable to make mistakes, they are just as fallible as the rest of us.

7. **It is okay to mourn a relationship you may never have.** It is human and natural to feel sad about that but don't let it define your life. Mourn but don't suffer!

8. **There is no one gold standard for a "normal relationship" with your parents.** This can vary for different people depending on what they value, what their needs are and the experiences they have had with their parents so far.

9. **Sometimes it is healthier to go "no contact."** While this can be a traumatic and painful decision to make, sometimes it is better for our well-being to remove ongoing sources of trauma.

See also:
Chapter 17: Taking Stock of Your Influences
Chapter 27: Processing Childhood Experiences
Chapter 33: When Situations Seem to Repeat Themselves

Chapter 32: Financial Instability

Whether you have student loans, trying to save to move out, or just struggling to get started, feeling financially unstable really stinks. Here are some ideas for how to manage when you're in this situation.

1. **Know where your money is going.** We don't want to tell you for the thousandth time to make a budget but make a budget. It doesn't have to be perfect, but just a sense of how much money is coming in and how much is going out. Sometimes just writing it down will help you see areas where you might want to make changes.

2. **What is important to you?** Some people are perfectly happy living paycheck to paycheck as long as they can do the things that are fun to them. Others want to save and plan and reach certain goals. Often it comes down to instant gratification vs. delayed gratification – and which is more important to you?

3. **Investing in yourself.** Many employers have matching investments to a retirement plan – take advantage of that as much as possible. You may also have other areas where spending money is a good investment, such as on your brain (with books or classes), your body (with good food or exercise), or your family. Once you clarify what is important to you, ensure your money is going there instead of to things that may be shiny but are not important.

4. **Can you cut your spending?** A good start is not charging anything on a credit card and only using available cash to make purchases. You can also examine any subscriptions or ongoing payments to see if you can reduce or eliminate those.

We aren't saying you have to stop buying coffee, but many of us have some wiggle room in our expenses where we could make small changes that add up.

5. **Can you increase your income?** This may seem like a silly question, but there are often opportunities for side hustles, part time jobs, or other ways to increase income, which can then be used to pay down debts. You can sell things you're no longer using on eBay or Craigslist. Of course, it's not ideal, but if a year of working weekends can get you debt free, that might be a good bargain!

6. **What are your patterns?** Sometimes people go shopping because they're bored. Or they buy a bunch of junk food, even though they want to get in better shape. Or they spend a lot of money going out with "friends" they don't even like that much. If you can identify patterns of spending money that serve you and patterns that don't serve you, you can start to make some changes. It's time to break those bad habits and start making new ones!

7. **Credit scores are serious.** Credit scores are a numerical calculation of your creditworthiness based on an analysis of your credit files, typically obtained from credit bureaus. High credit scores can make the difference in whether you are approved for a loan, such as a mortgage or a car; lower credit scores may mean you are offered worse terms (higher interest rates) for the loan or may mean you don't get the loan at all. It's a good idea to know your credit score, and to follow good money guidelines to obtain or maintain a good score, such as paying your bills on time.

8. **Student loans stink.** No doubt about it, student loans are awful. It feels like you'll be paying them forever. You may

want to explore repayment programs, particularly if you're in science, engineering, or medical fields. You might also consider refinancing the loans to get a special program, such as if you pay them for a period of time and then they are forgiven. Student loans do not go away with bankruptcy, so that's not a good choice.

9. **Beware quick fixes.** Plenty of places will promise to pay off your loans (and saddle you with theirs) or fix your credit report (for a big fee). The main way to fix the situation is by managing your earning and spending. It takes time, and there's no easy fix.

10. **Bankruptcy is a very last-chance option.** Declaring bankruptcy may seem like a good option, but it can also create more burdens, because you may have a trustee reviewing your finances and won't have good credit for years. Definitely talk to a lawyer if you are even considering this.

See also:
Chapter 6: Thinking Long-Term
Chapter 17: Taking Stock of Your Influences
Chapter 20: Choosing or Changing Careers

Chapter 33: When Situations Seem to Repeat Themselves

Apophenia is a human tendency to see patterns and seek meaning. While this isn't always for related things, we often tend to have specific ways we interact with the world and seeking relationships with people which may lead to a Groundhog Day style situation where situations appear to repeat themselves.

1. **Think about situations that are repeating.** Break down the series of choices or actions that seem to lead to these situations.

2. **See if you can identify any patterns** in these situations repeating themselves and the different parts of those patterns.

3. **Identify if any of those parts are in your control** and recognize your own agency and responsibility in those situations.

4. **Think about what other choices** you can make about the things that are in your control.

5. **Try alternatives in the moment.** If you identify actions or decisions on your part that contribute to the situations repeating themselves, try something different to help break that cycle.

6. **Recognize that you ultimately only have control over your own actions,** and that other people will still make their own choices.

7. **Focus on the things that you can do differently in the situation.** That can help you feel more in control and potentially change the outcome.

8. **If you know parts of repeating situations are going to be stressful** – have a plan in place for self-care after.

See also:
Chapter 1: Who Am I?
Chapter 6: Thinking Long-Term
Chapter 10: Understanding Your Own Thoughts, Feelings, and Desires

Part VII. Family, Friends, and Romantic Relationships

Chapter 34: Being Kind to Others

Human beings are social creatures, and our lives are heavily influenced and defined by the interactions we have with the people around us. Kindness and compassion go a long way in developing healthy, empathetic relationships grounded in reciprocity and mutual wellbeing.

1. **Remember that other people are also human beings** with their own hopes, fears, and motivations.

2. **Treat people with compassion.** Approach people with kindness even if you don't understand their actions.

3. **Be empathetic.** Try to understand where the other person is coming from in a situation.

4. **Develop your own communication style and be willing to be flexible.** Knowing how to effectively communicate with others will help guide your communication with them.

5. **Be honest.** You can be honest without being mean.

6. **Boundaries are a kindness.** Setting and communicating your boundaries with others helps people know where you stand with them and how to best support you.

7. **Avoidance doesn't help,** sometimes the kindest thing to do to maintain and nurture a relationship is having a difficult conversation.

8. **Be patient with others.** If you find yourself getting heated or worked up in a hard conversation, take a breather and come back to it when you are both calm.

9. **Remember to offer yourself the same kindness you offer others.** Sometimes we are our own worst critics. Showing compassion to yourself can help you stay grounded.

See also:
Chapter 1: Who Am I?
Chapter 3: Assessing Your Strengths
Chapter 26: Building a Better World Through Diversity, Equity, and Inclusion

Chapter 35: What to Share With Family, Friends, and Co-Workers

Sharing information and experiences is a vital part of developing health and fulfilling social relationships. It can help foster positive social interactions and lead to better cohesiveness and reciprocity in social, family, and professional groups.

1. **Know what you want to share with the different groups in your life.** There are so many people who are part of our larger community and not all these groups are connected.

2. **Everyone doesn't need to know everything about your life,** it is okay to selectively share information with different groups.

3. **What is the purpose of sharing?** It is okay to share whatever you'd like with different people. It's also good to be aware of why you're trying to share that information. Are you hoping for validation? Feedback? Just celebration? Identify your own personal motivations.

4. **Know how sharing information can impact your relationships.** Depending on the nature of the information you're sharing, realize that it may change your relationship. For example – sharing a promotion with a struggling coworker might negatively impact that dynamic. Alternately, sharing a traumatic experience with someone who is currently experiencing something similar could help strengthen that bond.

5. **Know other people's boundaries** and be respectful of them.

6. **Be mindful of the appropriateness of conversation topics.**
    Know the rules and expectations of the setting you are in.

7. **Timing of sharing can be incredibly important,** be mindful of
    when you're sharing information for the most effective
    communication.

8. **What you can share with others depends on the relationship
    you have with them.** This is something that can change over
    time and circumstances. Generally, it's not good to share a
    story that isn't yours.

9. **Respect your own privacy too.** Some things are okay to not
    share too if they cross your boundaries.

See also:
Chapter 28: Family Expectations of You
Chapter 38: Coming to Terms With Work
Chapter 43: Taking Responsibility for Yourself

Chapter 36: Engaging in Romantic Relationships

We've all been fed a line about finding "The One." This is the soulmate, the one person who will meet all your needs and be a best friend, spouse, and lover all in one. It works out like that for some of us, but many times pursuit of "The One" can blind us to many other good relationships. Here's some of the things you'll want to consider about romantic relationships.

1. **Emotional maturity.** Everyone has some flaws and emotional baggage, but we each need to carry our own. Making sure you're at equivalent emotional stages is important.

2. **Do the two of you have the same values and life plans?** If you're thinking house and kids and they are wanting lots of solo travel, this may not be a great match.

3. **Are you both looking for the same kind of relationship?** When they want a fling and you're looking for forever, it's not the right relationship.

4. **Pay attention to how you feel about yourself when you're with them.** If you feel better about yourself, that's awesome. If you're trying to please or impress, that's a big no.

5. **Openness, honesty, and respect are vital** no matter what kind of relationship you're looking for, and if it's not there, it's not "the one".

6. **Independence and the appreciation of some "alone time" are important.** You don't need to be joined at the hip 24/7, and

healthy relationships work best when you have both overlapping and separate interests.

7. **Pay attention to the degree and type of physical affection that you are looking for vs. what you're getting.** Major differences in this area can be cause for later dissatisfaction.

8. **If you're having sex, make sure it's working for both of you.** This includes frequency, intensity, duration, and type. Going out of your comfort zone is okay, but you don't want to feel pressured, uncomfortable, or uneasy.

9. **Having a similar sense of humor.** The ability to make each other laugh and having fun together is a wonderful counterbalance to the stressors that come up in life.

10. **Do they have friends?** How does it go when they're with their friends (or the two of you are with your friends)? Do you like their friends? Do they get along with your friends?

11. **Are they willing to work through disagreements and challenges?** Do they disagree diplomatically or is every disagreement a big blow up? Are they willing to compromise?

12. **Ask yourself if they are empathic and kind.** This is connected to emotional support and validation, which we all need at times. It's long been said that how people treat waitstaff and other servers says a lot about their personality.

13. **Pay attention to the ways they express or look for emotional intimacy and think about your own needs for intimacy.** There's always room for growth and learning about each other, but a lack of perceived intimacy hurts a relationship.

14. **Be patient!** Lasting, healthy relationships don't magically develop overnight. Those early pheromones may make it seem perfect but give yourself (and the relationship) a chance to grow before deciding this person is "The One."

See also:

Chapter 24: Avoiding Cults and People Who Will Take Advantage of You
Chapter 33: When Situations Seem to Repeat Themselves
Chapter 37: Who to Surround Yourself With

Chapter 37: Who to Surround Yourself With

Making and keeping friends as an adult isn't necessarily the easiest thing. Over time, our interests and values change, and it is important to surround ourselves with people who bring out the best in us.

1. **Identify who you spend time with.** Many people have said that we are the total of the five people we spend the most time with; who are these people for you? Do they share your values? Are they happy with their lives?

2. **There are lots of ways to meet more people.** Talk to your existing friends about meeting some of their friends. Work is an excellent place to meet friends and is often the most common way people expand their social circle. Think about the activities that interest you (or that you've considered but never done) and take a class or join a group. Book clubs are a great way to meet people and are an accessible way to increase your circle. The Meetup app has a wide variety of activities; consider trying something you wouldn't normally do! Using a co-working space is another way to meet people and get work done. Check out local options for volunteering as an opportunity to help others while meeting new people. Get to know your neighbors. Consider meeting people at church, temple, mosque, or another faith-based organization. If there's a speaking club in your area such as Toastmasters, you can improve your confidence in public speaking and make friends.

3. **Make a commitment to accepting invitations** (even when you're not in the mood) and to take the initiative to start

conversations. Getting out of your comfort zone can lead to good friends. If you're an introvert, you can feel brave by going out!

4. **Practice your social skills via online events.** Meetup, Toastmasters, and networking groups have online meetings. Sometimes just showing up and saying hello is enough for one night. Who knows? You might want to follow up with someone after the meeting.

5. **Determine if the people you meet are people you want to spend time with.** Not everyone you meet will become your best friend, and it's okay to have friends who are just "book club" friends. Someone might be a keeper if you share values, if you communicate clearly and easily, if you feel good when you're with them, and if you genuinely care about each other.

See also:
Chapter 4: Building a Support Team
Chapter 17: Taking Stock of Your Influences
Chapter 35: What to Share With Family, Friends, and Co-Workers

Part VIII. Coming to Terms With Reality and Taking Responsibility for Yourself

Chapter 38: Coming to Terms With Work

Work is an important and significant part of most people's lives. When you spend about 8 hours a day somewhere, almost half of your awake time, it tends to form a major part in your day to day living. Successfully navigating work and workplace politics, and developing your professional network is a useful skill to develop.

1. **Developing your professional network is an ongoing process.** Knowing other professionals in your field of work can be invaluable in making progress in your career.

2. **Understand your work values.** Just as you identify and develop a personal value system, knowing what is important to you will also help you nurture professional ethics that align with your core values.

3. **Figure out what you want from your job.** This can include the compensation, your job duties, whether the work is remote or in-person, independent or team-based and the overall work culture. Identify what are your must-haves, and what you might be willing to compromise on.

4. **Maintain a cordial relationship with your coworkers and identify your allies.** Having a contentious relationship with someone you work with can make your job challenging. Knowing your support system at work can provide a sense of security.

5. **Foster your relationship with your supervisor.** A good supervisor can be an incredibly useful mentor in helping you navigate your professional growth at the organization and in

the field of work. They can provide helpful feedback and give you the tools to move towards your goals.

6. **Use your strengths at work.** Demonstrate what you are good at when you have the opportunity – whether it is a specific task or a particular skill that helps you best manage your projects.

7. **Explore options to make the job what you want it to be.** Have a conversation with your supervisor and other leadership in your organization. Identify what is needed to make your day-to-day job exciting, challenging and fulfilling for you and explore whether it is possible to move into that kind of role within the organization or somewhere else.

8. **Maintain appropriate boundaries at work.** Bringing up sensitive topics of conversation or oversharing can be viewed as unprofessional based on your organization's values.

9. **Accountability matters.** When you make a mistake, acknowledge it, and take accountability for it. Have a plan to not repeat it going forward. This helps others view you as trustworthy and mature.

10. **Sometimes just take a deep breath** and focus on next steps.

11. **Have a plan.** It is good to be organized and have an idea of your day-to-day tasks, and long-term projects so you can manage your workload effectively.

12. **Sometimes, flexibility is required.** Work crises occasionally come up, and while having a plan is great, it is important to be flexible and be able to prioritize in the moment on how to move forward.

13. **Effective time management is self-care!** Know what your abilities are and prioritize your tasks for long-term sustainability.

14. This is a very brief overview; you can also check out our other books, *Millennials' Guide to Work*, *Generation Z's Guide to Work*, and *Millennials' Guide to Management and Leadership*.

See also:

Chapter 39: Coming to Terms With Your Body

You get only one body, so keeping in touch with its needs and keeping it healthy is vital to living. Some of us are taught that our bodies are too big, too small, too ... whatever. Over time, developing a positive relationship with our bodies is important to getting our shit together.

1. **Know your relationship with your body.** Touch base with how you're feeling and what is going on within you.

2. **Navigating society's expectations can be challenging,** particularly if you do not fit into the box that society says you should fit into.

3. **There are different standards of beauty all over the world.** Even if you don't fit in with any conventional beauty standards of today's world, you are beautiful! These standards have changed hundreds of times and will continue to change and are a superficial view of humans.

4. **Work on maintaining your health.** Sustainability and moderation in dietary and exercise choices provides the most ongoing and lost lasting benefits.

5. **Rest and relaxation are important.** Self-care can come in many forms and finding the most effective way for you is important for your wellbeing.

6. **Touch base with your body's needs.** Our body can be very effective as telling us what it needs.

7. **You may experience physical symptoms of mental distress.** Stress, anxiety, depression can often manifest in the form of physical symptoms such as racing heart, palpitations, low energy, insomnia, etc. If you need to see a physician, please do so.

See also:
Chapter 6: Thinking Long-Term
Chapter 14: Exercise
Chapter 43: Taking Responsibility for Yourself

Chapter 40: Coming to Terms With Your Living Situation

Your living situation is an incredibly important aspect of your day to day living. Having a safe, comfortable home space is vital to your wellbeing. There are many different aspects to consider when taking stock of your living situation and figuring out how to navigate challenges that come up. Below are just some of the things to consider when thinking about your living situation.

1. **Take stock of who you live with.** Are they just roommates? Friends? Family? Recognizing the relationship you have with the people you live with is vital in guiding your interactions with them.

2. **Identifying what you value in a living space.** This can include the amount of space you have, the level of privacy and the style of your living situation.

3. **Is it temporary or long term?** Knowing how long this living situation is going to be can help you best approach any challenges you might face. Note: If you are experiencing homelessness or a volatile living situation, www.211.org or calling 211 in the U.S. can help you connect with resources.

4. **Know what your must-haves in a living situation are.** For example, if you have a pet you want living with you, finding a pet friendly place and not having the people living with you be allergic to said pet would be must haves.

5. **Somethings maybe negotiable.** Have a clear conversation with the people you are living with about your expectations about your living space and any shared spaces so you can be on the same page.

6. **Your relationship with roommates.** Sometimes roommates are friends, and sometimes they are just roommates. Have clear communication with your roommates about how you would like your relationship to be to help have a respectful and cordial living space – it can be awkward to live with someone who makes your living space uncomfortable.

7. **Navigating living with family.** For some people, living with family as an adult can be awkward if they do not respect your privacy or desires around your living space. Ongoing respectful communication about what is working and what is not can help make the situation less challenging.

8. **Communicate about your schedule** – when are you likely to be home or not, if you are leaving for an extended trip, etc. It is just a common courtesy to offer people you share living space with if it might affect them.

9. **Discuss tasks around the home** – how will chores be distributed? Will you or others be doing home projects? How will you approach anything that requires fixing?

10. **Have a long-term plan for your housing.** It is okay to not have all the details worked out but knowing how you'd like your ultimate living situation to look like can help you work towards it.

See also:

Chapter 22: Should I Move Around or Settle Down
Chapter 24: Avoiding Cults and People Who Will Take Advantage of You
Chapter 37: Who to Surround Yourself With

Chapter 41: Coming to Terms With Social Media

Adults have always been worried about the influence of technology on younger people. They thought radio would be divisive, they though television would rot our brains, Walkmans (cassette players with headphones) would make us walk into traffic, and social media would make us detach from reality. Although we are still alive despite these technologies, we may not realize the impact they have on us. Here's how to consider how technology and social media affect us, and what to do if it does.

1. **What technologies and social media are you using?** Most of us are using laptops, phones, email, and streaming services for movies and shows. If you're on social media, are you on Facebook, Instagram, Twitter, TikTok, Mastodon, Reddit, or other services? A quick inventory may surprise you!

2. **How much time do you spend on these?** Some of us are glued 24/7 to our phones, checking our friends' Instagram; others of us only check periodically to see updates. Of course, our frequency of attention may vary depending on whether there's a big social or political event happening. However, much time you spend on these services, is that okay with you? Do you wish you spent more time or less time on them?

3. **What do you tend to spend time on when you're on social media?** There are areas of social media that are positive and create happiness, such as sites with cute puppies or kittens. There are also educational sites that provide explainer threads. The negative side of social media is that there are many places

online where you find hostility, racism, sexism, body shaming, and just plain meanness. Do you spend your time looking at areas of social media that are positive or ones that are negative?

4. **How do you feel when you spend time on social media?** Numerous studies have shown that after people spend a lot of time on social media, they are more likely to experience depression, anxiety, loneliness, self-harm, and suicidal thoughts. Others report that spending time on social media promotes negative experiences such as feeling inadequate or unattractive. How do you feel when you spend time on social media?

5. **Do you feel trapped by social media?** Many times, people report feeling trapped: they don't feel good when they're on social media, but when they take a break from social media, they feel like they're missing out and excluded from what everyone is talking about. Do you experience nervousness or anxiety when you are not on social media? Do you worry that people are talking about you or having fun without you?

6. **What is important to you?** Here's the sticky question: What do you want to prioritize in your life? Keeping up with the Kardashians or other celebrities or your friends? Seeing all the ways online in which you're not living up to a perfectly Instagrammed (and carefully curated) life? Or do you have priorities of spending time in real life with friends, family, educational goals, or other pursuits? How are your social media habits and behaviors contributing to your priorities?

7. **What, if anything, would you like to change about your time on social media?** Maybe it's blocking negative or harmful sites.

Maybe it's not spending as much time on social media or limiting which sites you go to. Maybe there are bigger issues, such as who you are friends with, or how you feel about yourself. Whatever you decide to do, consider what will contribute to the healthiest and happiest *you*.

8. **Set a goal for yourself and stick to it.** You can do this. Set a timer, close accounts, block connections, go cold turkey and block your accounts, or do whatever you have to do. Focus on what you're gaining and enjoy living!

See also:
Chapter 11: Online Support Groups
Chapter 17: Taking Stock of Your Influences
Chapter 25: Making Sense of the World Around You

Chapter 42: Coming to Terms With Your History So You Can Move Forward

Embracing all parts of past experiences, good and bad is essential in moving forward. Your history shapes who you are as a person and how you interact with the world. Coming to terms with your history can be challenging. Here are some helpful aspects to navigate this process.

1. **Integrating challenging experiences in your life.** Processing traumatic experiences in your life can help make meaning of those and help you know yourself, your value system, and your motivations better.

2. **Reconciling your choices with your value system.** Sometimes you might have had to make decisions that did not feel right but were necessary in the moment. It is okay to acknowledge that this wasn't something you would normally do but did in that specific situation. Acceptance of our past helps guide future choices.

3. **Sometimes it is not a "but" situation – it is an "and" situation.** Sometimes conflicting things can exist simultaneously. Recognizing that can help validate your experience.

4. **Situations are rarely black and white when humans are involved;** every different perspective is a shade of gray in between.

5. **Therapy can be helpful for making sense of trauma.** It can be a safe space to process experiences and develop health coping skills to navigate them going forward.

6. **Stages of processing your history can feel like the stages of grief.** You may experience denial, anger, bargaining, depression, and finally acceptance. It's okay. A therapist can help if you are struggling.

7. **If your past experiences were traumatic,** mourning is part of processing those.

8. **As with grief,** ultimately healthy processing of experiences leads to acceptance of things that cannot be changed.

9. **These experiences can be instrumental in shaping your value system** and how you respond to situations.

10. **Ultimately, be kind to yourself.** You have value as a human being and deserve love and respect.

See also:

Chapter 43: Taking Responsibility for Yourself

Adulting is hard. We are encouraged to take responsibility for ourselves, and sometimes that's not fun at all! But the good part is … we get to take responsibility for ourselves, and that can be an absolute joy. Let's walk through what it means to take responsibility for yourself.

1. **What does it mean to take responsibility?** Taking responsibility means you understand that you have a role in each situation and that in some way, the outcomes or consequences are related to your actions or inactions. We can get upset with our weight, but we hopefully can also see how our own habits around diet, sleep, exercise, and health have contributed to our weight. Owning up to our role, clarifying what we want to happen, and working toward that is part of taking responsibility and being accountable.

2. **At the same time, we can't be responsible for everything.** When we start taking responsibility, it's easy to start viewing everything as up to us. But none of us are all-powerful! The key to taking responsibility is understanding what we can impact and what we can't and making choices accordingly. That means we seek to impact the things we can change, and we don't beat ourselves up for the things we can't change. As the Serenity Prayer indicates, it takes wisdom to know the difference between what we can and can't change.

3. **What level of responsibility is right for you?** Some of us have had to take responsibility for ourselves early in life, such as doing our own laundry, making meals for ourselves, and getting ourselves up for school as children and teenagers.

Others of us have support from parents in paying bills and helping us solve our problems well into our 30s or 40s. As you are figuring out how you want to approach responsibility, it helps to understand how other people consider responsibility and what it means to them. Start asking! You can ask your friends if they had chores as kids, who was responsible for what in their family, and how they manage responsibility now. How are their experiences different from or similar to yours?

4. **Satisfaction of doing something on your own is its own reward.** Sometimes when you're struggling, it's hard to see a positive outcome. I (JPW) struggled to pay for my education, and several wise people told me that I would be so proud of myself later for doing it myself instead of having it handed to me. It took years to see the truth in their statements, but I am proud of myself for working through it.

5. **How do you get started being responsible?** When something happens that you don't like, ask yourself, "Is there any way I contributed to this?" You can consider that if you were to take responsibility what that would look like. Another way to increase responsibility is to stop blaming others.

6. **It's not about blame.** It's a fine balance here: the goal isn't to always find someone to blame. It's to step up and do what needs to be done. Blaming others is counterproductive. Even if it was someone else's error that got us here, approaching the situation to find solutions and resolve problems is a much healthier approach.

7. **Responsibility includes acceptance.** Acceptance is so hard! It means that you get that sometimes things won't go your way. Sometimes you won't get what you want. Sometimes you can't solve the problem or make it better. Sometimes it's your

responsibility that the thing happened, and sometimes it's no one's fault. Practicing acceptance can help you practice taking responsibility.

8.   **Responsibility also includes believing in yourself.** When you believe you can change and grow and improve, it's easier to take responsibility when you goof up. You're not defined by your mistakes, but by how you choose to approach life.

See also:
Chapter 1: Who Am I?
Chapter 3: Assessing Your Strengths
Chapter 6: Thinking Long-Term

Acknowledgements

The authors would like to thank Valerie Weaver for her initial thoughtful discussions about this book, and Gerry Vogel for reviewing and editing.

About the Authors

Sphoorti Pandit-Kerr, MA, is a Millennial who grew up in Mumbai and is now navigating the Pacific Northwest, living with her husband and two 80-pound lap dogs. She has a master's degree in psychology and more than a decade of working in research, community-based health care, and creative settings – all of which have had dealings with stressed out community members. She is an avid traveler and has been influenced by everywhere, everyone, and everything she has ever interacted with. She enjoys connecting with people, creative writing, visual arts, and is particularly passionate about "do-as-I-do-not-as-I-say" advice. She can be most often found either curled up with a book and a cup of coffee or trying to be 3 places at once.

Jennifer P. Wisdom, PhD MPH ABPP, is an author, consultant, speaker, psychologist, and principal of Wisdom Consulting. As a consultant, she helps curious, motivated, and mission-driven professionals to achieve their highest potential by identifying goals and then providing them with the roadmap and guidance to get there. Jennifer is the author and founding publisher of the *Millennials' Guides* series, including *Millennials' Guide to Work*, *Millennials' Guide to Management & Leadership*, and *Millennials' Guide to Diversity, Equity & Inclusion*. She lives in New York City. www.leadwithwisdom.com.

Additional Books by the Authors

Millennials' Guide to Work
Jennifer P. Wisdom

Millennials' Guide to Management and Leadership
Jennifer P. Wisdom

Millennials' Guide to Workplace Politics
Mira Brancu and Jennifer P. Wisdom

Millennials' Guide to Relationships
Kristina M. Hallett and Jennifer P. Wisdom

Millennials' Guide to Real Estate
Zachary Brickner and Jennifer P. Wisdom

Millennials' Guide to Diversity, Equity, and Inclusion
Lisa D. Jenkins and Jennifer P. Wisdom

Millennials' Workbook on Diversity, Equity, and Inclusion
Lisa D. Jenkins and Jennifer P. Wisdom

Generation Z's Guide to Work
Nora del Rosario and Jennifer P. Wisdom

Millennials and Generation Z Guide to Voting
Jeremy Levine and Jennifer P. Wisdom

Millennials' Guide to the Construction Trades
Karl D. Hughes and Jennifer P. Wisdom

Generation Z's Quick Guide to Leaving Home
Denise Zorer, Diana Polus, and Jennifer P. Wisdom

Millennials' Quick Guide to Being a Boss
Jennifer P. Wisdom

Millennials' Quick Guide to Money
David Mohammed and Jennifer P. Wisdom

www.ingramcontent.com/pod-product-compliance
Lightning Source LLC
Chambersburg PA
CBHW071151120626
46546CB00006B/2220